In Toronto, in April 1975, ̲ ̲Canadians and one American each presented a paper at a conference on what has become the key issue in current industrial relations – collective bargaining in the essential and public service sectors.

This book presents those papers along with transcripts of the substantial and lively discussions that followed each one and involved many of the leading Canadian figures in this field. The status of government employees is one of the most prominent of the issues discussed.

The speakers, Ben Aaron, University of California, Jean Boivin, Université Laval, James Matkin, Government of British Columbia, and Paul Phillips, University of Manitoba, deal with the causes of unrest in the essential and service sectors of the economy, the interrelationship of market and political forces, the results of various forms of government intervention, and also with international comparison of procedures for dispute settlement.

There was a considerable diversity of opinion expressed, yet there emerged from the discussions a sense of agreement as to which policies should be followed and those that definitely should not. The debate on collective bargaining in the essential and public sectors is current in legislatures and elsewhere. This work will be helpful in advancing that debate and in encouraging the adoption of measures conducive to social harmony. It will interest students of industrial relations, all those involved in public and essential service negotiations and legislation, and members of the general public affected by the disputes and interested in their resolution.

The conference was organized by David Beatty and chaired by John Crispo, and the papers edited by Morley Gunderson, all of the University of Toronto.

MORLEY GUNDERSON, editor

Collective Bargaining in the Essential and Public Service Sectors

Proceedings of a conference
held on 3 and 4 April 1975,
organized by David Beatty
through the Centre for Industrial Relations
University of Toronto,
chaired by John Crispo

UNIVERSITY OF TORONTO PRESS
TORONTO AND BUFFALO

© University of Toronto Press 1975
Toronto and Buffalo
Reprinted in paperback 2017
ISBN 978-0-8020-2222-6 (cloth)
ISBN 978-0-8020-6283-3 (paper)

Library of Congress Cataloging in Publication Data
Main entry under title:

Collective bargaining in the essential and public service sectors.

1. Collective bargaining – Government employees – Canada – Congresses.
2. Labor disputes – Canada – Congresses. I. Gunderson, Morley, 1945-
II. Toronto. University. Centre for Industrial Relations.
HD8013.C23C63   331.89'041'35471   75-31677
ISBN 978-0-8020-2222-6 (bound)   ISBN 978-0-8020-6283-3 (pbk.)

Contents

David M. Beatty, University of Toronto
PREFACE / vii

John Crispo, University of Toronto
INTRODUCTORY REMARKS / 1

Jean Boivin, Laval University
COLLECTIVE BARGAINING IN THE PUBLIC SECTOR: SOME
PROPOSITIONS ON THE CAUSE OF PUBLIC EMPLOYEE UNREST / 3
Discussion / 17

Paul Phillips, University of Manitoba
COLLECTIVE BARGAINING DYNAMICS AND THE PUBLIC INTEREST
SECTOR: THE MARKET AND POLITICS / 37
Discussion / 54

James Matkin, Deputy Minister of Labour, British Columbia
GOVERNMENT INTERVENTION IN LABOUR DISPUTES
IN BRITISH COLUMBIA / 79
Discussion / 101

Benjamin Aaron, University of California at Los Angeles
PROCEDURES FOR SETTLING PUBLIC INTEREST DISPUTES IN THE
ESSENTIAL AND PUBLIC SECTORS: A COMPARATIVE VIEW / 121
Discussion / 145

John Crispo
CONCLUDING REMARKS / 157

LIST OF PARTICIPANTS / 161

DAVID M. BEATTY

Preface

The papers and proceedings contained in this volume emanate from a conference sponsored by the Centre for Industrial Relations at the University of Toronto on 3-4 April 1975. The Centre invited a relatively small number of recognized academics and senior governmental officials to discuss round a table the much publicized apparent breakdown in collective bargaining in the public and essential service sectors. It was our hope to analyse the appropriateness of a collective bargaining model for determining wages and working conditions in these sectors, to identify the critical deficiencies and imperfections in the bargaining models that now exist, and to offer suggestions and directions that legislators might follow to alleviate and ameliorate those difficulties. It is my belief that this volume confirms that our hopes for this conference were realized.

The papers that were presented at the conference by Professors Boivin, Phillips, Matkin, and Aaron examine, from different perspectives, various collective bargaining models which either exist or could be constructed for the public and essential service sectors. These models would preserve the right of the employees to participate in the determination of their wages and working conditions and at the same time protect the public's and interested third parties' legitimate interests. The papers necessarily provided the framework and touchstone for the discussion that followed by the participants. Thus Professor Boivin's analysis identifies, from the employee's perspective, some of the basic deficiencies perceived in the existing models as inhibiting and indeed undermining the realization of a mature and responsible bargaining relationship. Professor Phillips in his paper similarly probes for institutional defects in the existing bargaining models but carries his analysis through from the employer's or governmental perspective. In the latter two papers, and against the backdrop of the two preceding papers, Professors Matkin and Aaron offer quite diverse suggestions as to the appropriate methods and techniques by which some of the difficulties identified by Professors Boivin and Phillips can be rectified in whole or in part.

The proceedings indicate the participants to have a remarkable degree of consensus on certain basic premises and conditions that must be recognized and given effect to by any legislature intending effective and viable solutions to the deficiencies now perceived in the present models of collective bargaining. In the first place, and perhaps most fundamentally, there appears to be virtual unanimity that industrial conflict, in these or any other sectors, is simply a manifestation of, and not itself the basic cause of, the apparent breakdown in collective bargaining. Rather, the consensus appears to be that there are more basic and fundamental forces which threaten the viability of collective bargaining in these sectors. These more basic deficiencies are described more specifically by Professors Boivin and Phillips and by the participants in the discussions that follow their papers.

Equally fundamental, and perhaps more surprising, is the apparent agreement of this conference that the rather draconian response of simply prohibiting industrial conflict in the public and essential service sectors is naive, ineffective, and palpably short-sighted. More critically, there appears from this conference to be a general recognition that such solutions are in fact inimical to the very public and governmental interests which such measures on their face purport to protect. This general rejection of such simplistic solutions stems in part from the realization by virtually all of the participants that some degree of industrial conflict is inevitable and simply cannot be denied legislatively. Apart from threatening and undermining the community's respect for the law, such general prohibitions fail to recognize and take account of the very real political pressures which are inextricably interwoven in any bargaining model in these sectors. In many instances these pressures would result in the mere threat of an unlawful strike being potentially more destructive of the legitimate interests and security of the public by providing the employees with a powerful tool of coercion which is not available to those employees who are legally permitted to strike. Finally, recognizing that some of the industrial conflict that has been witnessed in these sectors in recent years can be attributed to the relatively short experience that both employees and employers have had with collective bargaining, many of the participants argued that simply to deny these employees the right to withdraw their services would be to overreact to a phenomenon which in part can be ascribed to a system passing through its adolescent years.

Given these considerations it is not surprising, as the discussions which follow Professor Matkin's and Aaron's papers portray, that most of the differences evident at the conference related to the most appropriate methods by which the potential adverse effects of industrial conflict in these sectors can be monitored, limited, controlled, and channelled. From the papers of Professors Matkin and Aaron, as well as from the participants' comments, a myriad of suggestions emerged as to how public security and well-being can be preserved while allowing public and essential service employees the right to participate fully in the process by which their wages and working conditions are determined. From very specific proposals such as voluntary arbitration, non-stoppage strikes, and emergency services, the papers and discussion consider the merits and limitations of various structural and procedural mechanisms through which legislatures may invoke such proposals. Thus one can perceive very real differences between the establishment by government of a formal agency to continuously monitor, assist, and ultimately control the effect of industrial conflict rather than simply its responding on an *ad hoc* basis to specific instances as they arise. Each of the suggested schemes and procedures is designed to ensure a minimum of interference with the security and well-being of the public, while at the same time permitting the parties the widest scope to resolve their differences. Given that each scheme and procedure has its inherent strengths and weaknesses, the selection of a specific proposal will likely depend more on philosophical and political ideology than on the intrinsic superiority of any one scheme.

From the response of the participants, the Centre for Industrial Relations is confirmed in its view that the format adopted for this conference lends itself uniquely to a rational and productive study of current problems of labour relations in Canada. It is our hope that this seminar will be the first in a series of similar conferences in which neutral governmental and academic persons can be brought together to discuss, in a dispassionate and detached forum, current issues of industrial relations. For the success of this first venture, I must extend thanks to all of the participants who contributed to the conference, to each of the Departments of Labour who assisted in the financing, and to the University of Toronto and the Canada Council without whose generous support this conference would not have been possible.

JOHN CRISPO

Introductory remarks

This is probably the most turbulent time we've had in Canadian industrial relations since 1946, when the new industrial unions were really testing their mettle for the first time. Thinking back to that era allows one to take some aid and comfort from the thought that perhaps what we're going through today, particularly in the public sector, is again a new form of unionism that is maturing and passing through, if you will, a kind of teething period, finding out just how strong it is. That's obviously an over-simplification, but I think it is an aspect of the current situation that merits some attention.

Over-all, as you all well know, Canada is now running one of the highest levels of industrial conflict in the western world. According to the media, only Italy was ahead of us last year, and if we work at it we might even put them in second place next year. I am not as disturbed by this record as many people are because, if you look back over the years, Canada has normally ranked near the top in terms of the proportion of lost time due to industrial conflict. The United States used to give us a better run for first place, but the labour movement in that country, having lain down and played dead for the last few years, isn't even competing with us anymore. The point is that we've always been up near the top, something due in large part to the nature of our industrial relations system. It hasn't been damaging or worrisome because for the most part strikes in the private sector and in the traditional areas of collective bargaining have been fairly organized and predictable. Big inventories have been built up before the strikes took place; workers have saved their money, and we've had long strikes without much disruption or inconvenience, let alone hardship.

There are, however, two or three dimensions to the current situation that merit discussion. I have to admit that I'm rather concerned about these new dimensions and therefore have some appreciation for the degree of public consternation and disquiet that's abroad in the land. Let me just briefly touch on those aspects that are somewhat new and different. The first is the fact that a much greater proportion of the strikes we are experiencing are occurring in the service sector of the economy and particularly in the public service sector where no stockpiling can take place. If the railways or postal services go on strike, it's very hard to allow for it; this is making us a little more vulnerable to interruptions that affect many more people and get them more agitated than steel or auto or even meat-packing strikes. In the public mind, at least, their dependence on certain services is giving rise to a feeling that there's an element of blackmail involved. Again, I wouldn't exaggerate this feature of the situation, but it seems to me that it does concern people.

Another disturbing dimension in the current situation is to be found in the growing proportion of illegal strikes. In this regard it seems to me that the public sector is establishing the patterns and precedents. It's going to be very interesting to see whether the degree of defiance of the law, which some people think is already out of hand, can be contained. Some would doubtless argue that the best way to eliminate illegal strikes is to make all strikes legal. I suppose that's one solution – get rid of the no-strike obligation and then anybody can strike anytime.

It is also certainly going to be interesting to see if the defiance of the law by the public services will spread, in a fairly pervasive sense, to the private sector.

JEAN BOIVIN

Collective bargaining in the public sector: some propositions on the cause of public employee unrest

The determining factor in avoiding (public sector) strikes will be the speed with which governments move to eliminate the causes of strikes and provide sound collective bargaining laws and improved wages and working conditions for their employees.

The preceding quotation comes from Edward B. Krinsky of the Wisconsin Employment Relations Commission[1] and, to a certain extent, it reflects my own view about what should be done to improve public sector labour relations in Canada. Whether this is feasible is a different story, but if most public officials would proceed with such an approach, many problems could be settled or at least better understood. This presentation will be based on similar premises and it will be structured as follows: I will first briefly restate what I call 'the quest for collective bargaining by public employees.' Then, I will try to identify the major causes of public employee unrest which I group into three broad categories: lack of collective bargaining laws, failure of governments or other types of public employer to provide adequate wages and working conditions, and inadequate impasse resolution machinery. Finally, I will try to circumscribe the limits within which any improvement to public sector labour relations can be achieved, and I will indicate some general principles which I consider important prerequisites to a sound public policy on the matter.

Although I have been asked to comment upon the over-all Canadian picture, it will be a material impossibility to make an in-depth analysis

Note references are located *after* the discussion of the paper; see p. 35.

of every jurisdiction's major problems. On the one hand, I must admit
that I only have a very formal knowledge of the situation prevailing
in some jurisdictions; on the other hand, so many changes have recently been introduced to the legislative framework within which collective bargaining takes place that it is too soon to know whether they
represent appropriate answers to today's problems. That is why my
comments will be general in scope with sporadic references being made
to particular experiences.

THE QUEST FOR COLLECTIVE BARGAINING

I suggest that the appearance of collective bargaining in the Canadian
public sector is a natural and inevitable by-product of a North American society which is committed to the goals of welfare capitalism and
which historically has had deep aversion for state intervention in the
economy. Hence, it is not necessary to rely on any political theory to
justify collective bargaining in the public sector, but rather on the
general factors which lead workers to form unions and to seek participation in the determination of their working conditions. These factors
are the same – with very few exceptions – in both the private and
public sectors, namely: the presence of socio-psychological and economic constraints at the work place. As the late E. Wight Bakke said:
'All the conditions and circumstances that have made employees ready
for collective bargaining in sectors where it has been established are
present in the employment relations of a critical mass of public
employees.'[2]

For Bakke, the predisposition to organization and collective bargaining becomes manifest under the following conditions: common
standards; absence of individual bargaining power; a situation where
the goods or services produced are social products in the sense that
there are several strata of supervision between the employee and the
decision-making employer; a situation where the 'employer' is in
reality another group of organized employees called 'management'; a
situation where there is an organized group support for a group spokesman which provides him with a regularized role that does not damage
his personal security; performance results dependent on management;
and a community of interest among the employees involved, such as
common skills and standards of performance, similarity in type and
extent of training, etc.[3]

Applied to the public sector, these factors can be considered as the result of more specific influences: advanced technology, extensive industrialization, and a different role played by the state in the economy which led to an over-all shift in the occupational profile of the labour force and to an increase in the 'size' of the public sector. However, the presence of these factors in the working situation was not enough. There also had to be the development of a group consciousness with a common purpose and common will.[4] White-collar employees such as teachers and government employees became more aware of their common interests as blue-collar workers had done thirty years earlier. Their pro-union orientation was late to come because of two basic motivations: they identified psychologically with management and, they considered themselves well treated by their employers. A large number of these workers were not class-conscious in outlook, nor were they collectivist in approach; rather they were individualistic and conservative. However, the new technology and its impact on the industrial structure was instrumental in fostering more favourable attitudes toward unions. And the change of outlook among government employees which grew out of the psychological factor of group consciousness facilitated the organization of many municipal workers, teachers, nurses, policemen, firemen, etc. Also important in the public employees' working situation was an increasing economic insecurity. Wage and fringe-benefit gains by unions in private industry, widely reported in the press, found a receptive audience among government workers. Long-standing local wage relationships between private and public employees were upset to the all too apparent disadvantage of the latter. At the same time the traditional 'security' of government employment looked less and less appealing in a progressively inflationary economy characterized by tight labour markets. This was particularly the case with the steadily growing number who entered government service in recent years. Finally, the usual methods by which public servants received wage increases were too cumbersome and uncertain, pointing up that new approaches were called for. As a result, the last decade experienced an upsurge in union membership at all levels of government which surprised not only public officials, but also those considered knowledgeable in labour matters.

CAUSES OF PUBLIC EMPLOYEE UNREST

Lack of adequate collective bargaining laws
Once public employees[5] opted for collective bargaining as the best

way to participate in the determination of their working conditions, they tried to convince public officials that the practice of collective bargaining should receive legislative approval in the public sector. Their rising militancy, as shown by the number of 'recognition' strikes, and their efficient lobbying activities finally defeated the sacrosanct principle of the sovereignty of the state in most jurisdictions of North America.

Nonetheless, the extent to which collective bargaining has been officially accepted is quite uneven throughout North America. For example, there are still some twelve states in the United States which have not enunciated either a right to organize or to bargain collectively.[6] Moreover, in some of them, until very recently, joining a union or an association was considered a sufficient cause for discharge. Fortunately, some test cases have now shown that the right to join an association was protected under the 1st and 14th amendments of the United States constitution.[7] On the other hand, some other states, like Indiana and Illinois, only tolerate collective bargaining in the absence of any legal statutes, while others have timidly recognized *some* public employees' right to 'meet and confer' with their employers.[8] And at the federal level, civil servants do not even have the right to bargain over their wages and salaries.

In Canada, the situation is not so bad. In the first place, municipal employees have enjoyed collective bargaining rights for a long time since, according to the Canadian constitution, municipalities are strictly creatures of the provinces and for labour relations purposes, they are considered as private employers.[9] Secondly, at the provincial level, all provinces have either adopted collective bargaining statutes for most categories of public employees or various inquiry commissions on public sector labour relations have recommended the adoption of such statutes. Finally, the federal government certainly does not lag behind any other public employers in North America – it granted genuine bargaining rights to its employees in 1967.

Even if the general acceptance of basic collective bargaining concepts seems to be better in Canada than in the United States, there remains the fact that there is no consistent pattern for the country as a whole. At one extreme, there are jurisdictions like Quebec, Manitoba, Saskatchewan, and recently British Columbia, which have granted full collective bargaining rights, including the right to strike, to some or all public employees. At the other extreme, there are jurisdictions where, although the principle of collective dealings between public employees and their employers has been accepted, the government either retains wide discretionary powers over the terms and conditions of employment (Newfoundland and Prince Edward Island) or considerably limits public sector unions' pressure tactics (Alberta, Ontario, Nova Scotia). The federal government and New Brunswick are somewhere in the middle in the sense that they have accepted the possibility of legalized pressure tactics while at the same time they have permitted bargaining agents to let a third party determine their working conditions.

Although one can agree with Ms Shirley Goldenberg that 'recent and anticipated changes all point in the same general direction – broader bargaining rights for government employees and a corresponding decline in absolute employer prerogatives,'[10] it is still true that many public employees, mostly at the provincial level, do not enjoy full collective bargaining rights. And, as long as they seek to achieve the 'private sector model,' their perception of the inadequacy of collective bargaining laws will remain as an important cause of unrest.[11] Such criticism by public sector unions does not rely only on the fact that many of them are deprived of the right to strike. It is also the result of a perceived 'double standard' treatment as regards the limited coverage of some collective bargaining statutes (teachers in Ontario, for example) or the limited scope of bargaining (like the classification system in most civil services systems).

Inadequate impasse resolution machinery
As a complement to the general criticism about the inadequacy of many collective bargaining laws, public employees are also dissatisfied with the present state of most impasse resolution mechanisms. This dissatisfaction seems somehow paradoxical since it comes as much from public employees whose labour relations are regulated by a very 'liberal' legislation (as in Quebec) as from public employees who are faced with a much more restrictive statute (hospital workers in Ontario, for example). In the first instance, the rationale behind the criticism relies on the fact that even if a similar impasse resolution procedure as the one which exists in the private sector applies to public sector employees, the provincial government always intervenes to hamper the latter's exercise of the legal right to strike. On the other hand, Ontario's hospital workers have harshly denounced the actual compulsory arbitration procedure and have started a campaign in order to obtain the legal right to strike. On the basis of the Quebec experi-

ence, it seems questionable whether Ontario's hospital workers are pursuing a desirable objective but, in any event, what matters the most is the fact that in both cases, there is growing dissatisfaction with the actual impasse resolution machinery.

I am less familiar with the degree of discontent prevailing elsewhere in Canada, but my personal feeling is that public employees are and will be more and more challenging impasse resolution procedures which basically rest upon third party determination of working conditions. And the fundamental reason explaining such discontent may not be the inadequacy of such procedures but the actual precarious economic situation which leads organized groups to take any means – legal or illegal – to protect the interests of their members. Because of this confusion, it is very difficult to assess whether impasse resolution mechanisms are adequate or not. The only thing that is certain is that they are going to be systematically criticized and used as scapegoats to explain many of today's labour relations problems.

For my part, I do not want to speak *ex cathedra* by trying to assess the sins of every jurisdiction's impasse resolution machinery. Two serious factors discourage such a course of action. On the one hand, the adoption of a specific type of impasse resolution procedure is so recent in many jurisdictions that it must first be given a chance to function for some time before it can be assessed adequately (such is the case in British Columbia, Alberta, Manitoba, Prince Edward Island, Newfoundland, and to a certain extent in Ontario with Bill 105). On the other hand, it is almost impossible to find appropriate standards to judge the adequacy of various impasse resolution procedures. Obviously, one could use the number of strikes – legal and illegal – but this would be a very short-sighted approach to the question. Indeed, although it may be true that the existence of a substantial number of illegal strikes in any one jurisdiction is probably a strong indication that the impasse resolution machinery is inadequate, the reverse is not so true. Moreover, since actual impasse resolution procedures are the product of a more or less general consensus among the population and compromises among the parties' divergent interests, any change cannot be introduced without first taking into consideration these two dimensions. That is why, it is ultimately those who have to live with the impasse resolution machinery who should decide on their own particular method. And given that the economic environment and socio-political values are not quite the same from one jurisdiction to another, a system which can be considered as adequate in one jurisdiction may be completely inappropriate in another.

There are three basic models for the settlement of interest disputes in Canada outside the municipal sector. The first is the compulsory arbitration model in Ontario, Alberta, Prince Edward Island, and the Manitoba and Nova Scotia civil services. The second is the right-to-strike model which is found in Saskatchewan, Quebec, Newfoundland,[12] British Columbia, and in Manitoba and Nova Scotia for employees other than civil servants. The third dispute resolution model is the 'choice of procedure,' where the bargaining agent must decide in advance whether it will choose compulsory arbitration or conciliation followed by the right to strike. This machinery is available to federal and New Brunswick civil servants. While the federal Act requires the bargaining agent to make its choice prior to commencing negotiations, the decision may be made at any time in New Brunswick and may actually be changed as negotiations proceed. It would seem from a public employee viewpoint that the New Brunswick procedure is much more flexible than the federal government's since it permits the bargaining agent to modify its decision according to any perceived variation in its bargaining power. In any event, the 'choice of procedure' model appears to be preferable than either of the other two models because it provides public employees who have very little bargaining power or whose services are so essential that they cannot use the strike weapon with a viable alternative to unilateral determination by public employers.

It is interesting to note that a procedure which has received a great deal of consideration in the United States – fact-finding – has been almost completely disregarded in Canada. I think this is a good illustration of the fact that the decision to adopt one type of impasse resolution machinery over another is a function of socio-political variables which are different from one jurisdiction to another. In the United States, the remnants of the old sovereignty doctrine are probably stronger than in Canada. The notions that one cannot strike against the state or that it is an unconstitutional delegation of sovereign authority to let a third party determine the terms and conditions of employment are still deeply rooted among large segments of the American population. For such people, a procedure like fact-finding which is not terminal and which places the final decision on the Legislature, conforms more to their socio-political values than does the right to strike or compulsory arbitration.

Failure of public employers to provide for
adequate wages and working conditions

Public employees all across Canada are now complaining that their wages and salaries have not kept pace with a rising cost of living even if, in absolute terms, they are much better off than they used to be ten years ago.

The fundamental reason justifying such discontent may appear to be the overall state of the economy which economists now character-ize as 'stagflation.' Although this factor should not be neglected, it is my belief that the source of discontent is more deeply rooted. In fact, I consider the following three factors as the major causes of pub-lic employee dissatisfaction with their level of remuneration: 1, the manner by which public services are financed and the ever-widening gap between revenues and responsibilities (and thus outlays) among the three levels of government; 2, the sacrosanct criterion of private sector comparability; 3, and the use of percentage increases which has the effect of widening the gap between lower and better paid employees.

1. At a time when lower levels of governments see their responsi-bilities considerably increased as a result of decisions which have often been taken by higher levels of authority (as has been the case with the creation of many urban communities), their revenues do not in-crease as much as the revenues of the federal and provincial govern-ments. Since municipal employers are also politicians and are the first to receive complaints about rising property taxes, they are reluctant to increase them still further to improve conditions of public employ-ees (which usually represent about 60 per cent of their budget). How-ever, given the greater vulnerability of municipal governments which are not 'sovereign' bodies, they are under strong pressure from both the labour unions and the taxpayers. If the municipal unions are mili-tant and if they have some political power, they will seek to precipi-tate an intervention from the provincial government, knowing very well that, in the end, it is at this level of authority that the decision about the financing of the settlement will be taken either through special grants or through the usual 'pass-the-buck' formula. Hence, the more or less favourable situation of municipal employees will de-pend upon the political pressure their unions can muster in negotia-tions. In this regard, however, all municipal employees are not in the same relative position vis-à-vis their employers.

On the other hand, the government which has benefited the most from increased tax revenues – the federal government – uses only 14 per cent of its budget to finance its wage bill. This government is nevertheless submitted to a different kind of constraint: the risk of creating precedents which other levels of governments cannot afford to follow.

Thus, whatever the level of government involved, there is growing dissatisfaction among public employees. Those governments which can afford to provide better working conditions don't for fear of being 'pattern-setters,' and those which have considerably less financial resources either frustrate the legitimate needs of their public employees or satisfy only a minority of them. In all instances, the direct consequence is increased union militancy.

2. At a time when public employees' wages and working conditions were substantially inferior to those of private sector employees, the achievement of some kind of parity with average private employers was a reasonable goal for many public sector unions. With the passage of time, after the necessary catch-up operation had been completed, the practice of relating public employees' salaries to those of taxpayers doing similar work nevertheless remained in force. As long as this formula yielded benefits which were judged acceptable by public employees, there was no problem. However, this system of public sector wage determination was plagued with two important shortcomings which were sooner or later bound to generate much unrest among public employees. First, there was likely to be disagreement between the employers and the unions over which reference group was going to be used for comparative purposes. Secondly, this procedure necessarily implied a time-lag which could be more or less lengthy according to the stability or instability of the economy.

The actual situation in many if not all jurisdictions across Canada is such that public employees are losing on both grounds. In Quebec, for example, public sector unions have for long abandoned the idea that public employees should be paid the private sector average. They want their members to be compared with the best employers. Such view is obviously in complete contradiction with traditional North American socio-political values, but it nevertheless reflects a specific conception of the state which, if accepted, perfectly justifies the unions' claim. This partially explains why the Quebec government must more and more resort to unilateral legislative action to enforce collective agreements: it is not ready to modify substantially the role of the state in the direction wanted by the unions.

On the other hand, even some public employees who have traditionally been less ideologically oriented, such as federal civil servants, have started to challenge the criterion of private sector comparability. Their major criticism is directed at the time-lag aspect of the procedure. They are no longer ready to come following after private employees. They want to do their own thing and create their own patterns. Should this challenge spread extensively across Canada, the whole wage determination system would be shaken up: and if the actual rate of inflation does not settle down, it is probably going to happen.

3. It has become an increasingly accepted policy within the Canadian labour movement to try to reduce salary differentials between low- and high-wage earners. The rationale behind this objective does not need to be explained in detail: inflation, among other things, has more disastrous consequences on low-wage earners than high-wage earners. None the less, the widespread practice in the past decade was to provide systematically for equal percentage increases of public employees' wages and salaries. Such practice, coupled with the private sector comparability criterion, has led to an ever-widening gap between lower and better paid employees. This widening is contrary to the general objective pursued by the labour movement.

Public sector unions, to a certain extent, are to be blamed for this situation. As the president of the Public Service Alliance of Canada admitted: 'Perhaps, in our anxiety to assure public servants wages *comparable* to those paid in the private sector, we have been a party to wage settlements for low-wage earners which, although statistically defensible, were morally outrageous.[13] Mr Edwards qualifies this percentage increase syndrome as 'a statistical camouflage for increasing distortion of the relative affluence of those in high income brackets and the relative deprivation of those in the lower brackets.'[14] I agree entirely with his opinion.

Fortunately, public sector union leaders are now aware of this situation and, one hopes that they will seek to remedy the situation. But in order to do so, they must first develop a consistent policy among themselves. As regards federal employees, I am not very optimistic about their success since the existence of some eighty bargaining units prevents the development of cohesive union solidarity. However, the situation is different in Quebec and New Brunswick where wider bargaining units favour the application of a more uniform bargaining policy.

Should most public sector unions be able to achieve this objective of reducing wage differentials, I believe that a great deal of unrest can be removed among many categories of public employees.

SOME SUGGESTIONS TO FOSTER THE DEVELOPMENT OF A SOUND LABOUR RELATIONS POLICY IN THE PUBLIC SECTOR

The purpose of this final section is to circumscribe the limits within which any improvement to public sector labour relations can be achieved and also to indicate some general principles which should guide the development of a sound public policy.

Two basic prerequisites
Before discussing the general principles mentioned above, I believe that the two following prerequisites – which are in fact two important limitations – should be accepted as inherent dimensions of the problem: 1, there is no viable alternative to collective bargaining as the best means to determine public employees' working conditions; 2, there is no universal solution to problems in public sector labour relations.

1. Whatever the criticisms raised against the collective bargaining institution either in the sense that it gives public employees a second crack at affecting the allocation of public resources (the first one being the usual lobbying activities displayed by public employee associations) or in the sense that it can jeopardize the public interest, we are condemned to accept it as the only practical way to permit public employees to participate in the determination of their working conditions in North America. There is just no viable alternative. For employees who have already been granted collective bargaining rights, their goal is to consolidate and extend these rights. For all others who do not already enjoy such rights, the objective is to obtain them.

On the other hand, public sector unions will never relinquish the degree of participation which they have achieved through collective bargaining in favour of any subtle form of consultation or any other devices short of collective bargaining. For their part, politicians would certainly have to think twice before they take the chance to permanently remove collective bargaining rights from a substantial portion of the labour movement.

2. I have already mentioned this point previously and I am just going to restate it briefly here. It would be foolish to try to devise a

universal system suitable to all jurisdictions. Solutions must be adapted to peculiar historical circumstances and to the specific needs of the parties concerned. In the end, we must accept that, when changes are introduced in the legal framework within which collective bargaining takes place, they are not the results of objective considerations but rather reflect the relative degree of political power which various interest groups possess within this jurisdiction. The adoption of a very liberal legislation vis-à-vis public employees as early as 1964 in the Province of Quebec was the direct consequence of an over-all sociopolitical reform at a time when the labour movement had a strong influence in government circles. The same considerations also apply to the recent situation in British Columbia and I think that anybody can think of many more similar examples.

General principles that should guide public policy
If we accept the position that collective bargaining in the public sector has passed the point of no return, I would favour the granting of full collective bargaining rights, including extensive coverage of the public sector labour relations statute,[15] wide rather than narrow bargaining units, extensive scope of bargaining, and a dispute settlement machinery which should leave the option between compulsory arbitration and the right to strike. I would also suggest that the structure of collective bargaining be such that it permits union negotiators to deal with the real and decisive sources of authority on the employer side.

This suggestion brings us to the delicate problem of distinguishing between the government as employer and the government as legislator. Theoretically, collective bargaining should occur between the unions and the government as employer with the government as legislator acting in a neutral capacity and as the final arbitrator. Even if legal structures have tried to isolate these two conflicting roles of government, experience has shown that it is almost impossible to dissociate them in practice. Ultimately, public sector unions' bargaining power is determined by their capacity to influence the government as legislator since, in the British parliamentary type of political democracy, the executive controls the legislative branch of government.

One good example illustrating this point occurs when the government enacts special legislation to put an end to a strike and/or unilaterally determines the terms and conditions of employment, as has now become a ritual in Quebec. Although the government seems to enjoy a considerable advantage vis-à-vis private employers because it can use the power of the law, it must nevertheless take into consideration possible adverse public reaction to its unilateral gesture. That is why, each time a government resorts to legislative action (such decision being commanded by the necessity to maintain essential services), it usually buys off the unions by granting them additional concessions which the latter could not get from the official employers' representatives at the bargaining table.[16]

Such apparently irrational concessions, from the standpoint of traditional collective bargaining theory, can only be explained by the political nature of public sector bargaining. Even if government can rely on its final authority as legislator and even if it is hard pressed by the population to restore essential services, there is something inherent in the political process which prevents or restricts the government from using its tremendous power.[17]

It would thus be useless to try to reduce the level of strike activity by simply bringing amendments to collective bargaining statutes which, at best, can only lead to a more or less adequate formula to maintain essential services, since the real factors affecting bargaining power ultimately rest outside the current industrial relations system. What should be recognized in the end is that the final solution to labour relations conflict in the public sector will always be a political one. From that perspective, we can only consider collective bargaining as 'a process for the mutual formulation of the public employee compensation package and related matters, before it is dropped into the legislative political arena to compete with other claimants for the allocation of public resources.'[18]

CONCLUSION

I conclude by reformulating my most important propositions:

1. Collective bargaining based on the private sector model has been and still is a target for most public employee unions. However imperfect, this is the only process which we have to resolve legitimately the question of public employees' participation into the determination of their working conditions. As the chairman of the New York State Public Employment Relations Board pointed out: 'It is not a particularly neat and tidy process, but neither are the tugs and hauls of public opinion which constitute the democratic system.'[19]

2. Most actual public employee unrest can be attributed to three major causes: a lack of adequate collective bargaining laws, a per-

ceived inadequacy in impasse resolution machinery, and economic insecurity. As long as public sector unions seek to achieve the 'private sector model' for collective bargaining, and as long as public officials deny them such rights, there will be militancy over the issue. As regards impasse resolution machinery, there is a growing tendency on the part of public sector unions to criticize any existing procedure. I believe that dispute settlement machinery is mostly used as a scapegoat and that the solution to public sector labour relations problems lies in much more complex factors.

3. Part of this solution comes from an amelioration of public employees' wages and working conditions. Ideally, the government should be made a model employer. But even if actual governments would be willing to play this role (which would imply that they accept to be pattern-setters instead of pattern-followers vis-à-vis the private sector), they would face serious difficulties because of the way financial resources and public responsibilities are shared among the three levels of government. On the other hand, public sector unions must put an end to the practice of uniform percentage increases which is widening the gap between lower and better paid employees.

4. If it is believed that an amelioration of the legal framework in which collective bargaining takes place can lead to improved labour relations, it must be recognized that there is no universal model which can fit any situation. Any improvement in impasse resolution machinery or in other aspects of the collective bargaining statute must be made in accordance with the parties' willingness to function within the system.

5. I would suggest that public officials take a relatively permissive attitude and grant public employees the most extensive collective bargaining rights possible (i.e., given the degree of public acceptability or tolerance vis-à-vis collective bargaining). This would remove an important cause of frustration on the union side.

6. Finally, given the highly political nature of public sector labour relations, I do not think that technical modifications to the collective bargaining statute – even the best ones – can be the final answer. We can have the best procedure to determine the manner in which essential services should be maintained or the best theoretical distinction between the respective roles of government as employer and government as legislator; however, if the unions feel that they can be better off by short-circuiting the system and if they have the power to do it, they will not behave according to expectations.

7. Hence, the actual situation can be depicted as follows: collective bargaining based on the private sector model represents an imperfect way of determining the public employee compensation package as can be seen from the shortcomings inherent in any incremental modifications of collective bargaining statutes. However, we have to stick with it because there is no viable alternative and because it would be politically unfeasible to replace it with something else.

DISCUSSION

Crispo It seems to me there were at least four things that you raised that we might focus on for discussion purposes. The first would be the question of whether there is any validity left to the old double standard that used to apply, and still does in some jurisdictions, to public employees. The second is the so-called catch up or pattern-following thesis that has historically applied to public servants. The third is dissatisfaction with working conditions, another major variable explaining the militancy we've seen in the public sector. The fourth is the political dimension of the problem and the question of whether in effect in the public sector we've substituted political pressures for economic pressures.

On this question of a double standard you have taken the very strong position that it is no longer appropriate, if it ever was, and that as far as you're concerned, workers in the public service, in Quebec if not elsewhere in Canada, are simply not going to accept any sort of double standard any longer. They want full-scale bargaining rights and they intend to get them, law or no law.

Johnston I find this question of double standard needs a little clarification. I had assumed from my reading of the article that really what we were talking about is whether we deny the public servants, for example, the right to strike. In other words, we deny them something that private sector employees have in the way of alternative methods of trying to resolve disputes. Or the other way of looking at the double standard is that in the public service we restrict the scope of bargaining in areas such as, for example, pensions at the provincial and federal levels. I hadn't assumed that a case was being made for separate legislation and administrative processes for running collective bargaining in the public area as distinct from in the private area. If this is the case then the problem is not whether the system is fair, but whether it is perceived as being fair, and I think it's true to say that the objective of a lot of public employee unions at the moment is to get the same treatment as the private sector. In Ontario, for example the CSAO and others would say their ultimate objective is to get under the Labour Relations Act.

Le Bel I must say that I am a little bit taken aback at the turn that this discussion has taken because, all along, I thought that Professor Jean Boivin was advocating that, inasmuch as possible, public sector employees be brought under private sector collective bargaining legislation. I thought he had emphasized, particularly when he pointed out that one of the problems was really the perceptions and aspirations of these employees, the fact that they resent the double standard or what they perceive to be the double standard. They find evidence of that double standard not only in specific restrictions that may be applicable to them but in the fact that they are under a different Act, under a different administration. Then, I heard my friend Jean Boivin say that, after all, he was in favour of a separate statute. I don't know where he stands right now. I agree with Mr Johnston. I think that we cannot do what Professor Boivin is suggesting, which would be moving towards the private sector legislation but tampering with it whenever it was felt to be convenient, such as with regard to the administration of the Act or the determination of the bargaining units. These are pretty basic issues. The determination of the appropriate bargaining units in the public sector has long been considered an almost insoluble problem.

I am now beginning to wonder whether the problem is all that different from what it is in the private sector – except that, of course, governments like to tamper with the rules and to set up the sort of system and bargaining structure which they want to deal with. For example, when the Public Service Staff Relations Act was enacted, it provided for a very special bargaining structure which was designed to achieve two objectives: to protect and perpetuate a classification system which had just been conceived and implemented by the federal government; and to maintain a certain pattern of staggered negotiations so as to allow the Treasury Board to preserve the existing two-year salary revision cycle.

If we are really concerned about this problem of double standard, we should face it and realize that the only way to do away with it is to bring all employees under the same legislation. Of course, just as many labour relations statutes contain special provisions for certain types of services or certain industries (fishing, construction, etc.), it may be necessary at certain steps in the process to include in the Act special provisions applicable to various groups of public employees. It may well be that one of the areas where this should be so is impasse-resolution procedure. However, I would suggest that if we are to en-visage that approach, we must start thinking about redefining the public sector.

The manner in which the public sector is presently defined in Canada bears no relationship to the public's idea of the public service. For example, throughout Canada, municipal workers and, generally, employees of public transportations systems in major cities fall under private sector collective bargaining legislation. Yet, for the average citizen, these employees provide a public service; when the citizens are confronted with the bus driver's strike, they do not care whether these employees fall under this or that legislation. In fact, the public cares a lot more about such strikes than if some clerks in a govern-ment go on strike. Yet, because various groups of public employees received collective bargaining rights at different times and because government employees have generally been treated as falling in a spe-cial category, these distinctions are perpetuated by the existing pattern of labour relations statutes. I do not think that we are going to re-solve that problem by maintaining two or more different collective bargaining statutes. Such an approach will not resolve the problem of the double standard and will further obscure the distinction bet-ween public and private by focusing solely on the identity of the employer instead of on the nature of the service. And I think that this is a key problem.

Aaron I think that the question raised by Professor Boivin does raise some particular problems in the United States. Basically, the problem arises from the different traditions of the common law and the civil law. In the private sector in the United States, substantive terms of employment are established by direct bargaining and as a matter of contract rather than as a matter of law. But when you move into the public sector, you begin to see a model that is very similar to that found in the continental European countries, namely, normative con-ditions prescribed by law which are non-waivable. This means that, in the event collective bargaining becomes established in the public sector, the immediate prospect is for whatever benefits to public sector employees that may result from the bargaining simply to be added to whatever minimum benefits have already been established by law. In the current debates over the proposed collective bargaining law for public employees in the State of California, for example, these ideas come directly into conflict; I'll give just one illustration. The proposed law is to be applied comprehensively to all public employees, including teachers. Now the employment conditions currently applicable to teachers are set forth with great particularity in the California education code. And the bill in its present form proposes that collective bargaining agreements, to the extent that they are inconsistent with local ordinances or charter provisions, shall take precedence. In other words, the local ordinances and charter provisions in the various cities can be disregarded by mutual agreement of the parties, provided, of course, that their agreement is approved by the appropriate legislative body. But that provision does not extend to state legislation; and so the school boards which are governed by the education code complain bitterly that they would be forced by this proposed legislation to bargain with one arm tied behind them, so to speak. In other words, all the minimum conditions would still prevail and all they could do would be to grant something more. What they seek is the right to bargain over such matters as: the authority summarily to discharge teachers who participate in an illegal strike instead of having to wait five consecutive days, as provided in the education code; the issue of tenure; prevailing wage requirements; and the like. What appears to be the case is that the public employees, while decrying the present double standard applicable to the public and private sectors, are arguing, in effect, for its continuance in those respects favourable to themselves. They want to keep what they already have without the risk of having to bargain it away for something else in the course of negotiations. And to give one final example, the police and firemen simply do not want the right to strike, which is being proposed in a limited way; they aren't even willing to accept the onus of declaring publically that they *may* strike. They want absolutely to be told that they may not strike and that they are entitled instead to compulsory arbitration. The other public employees, on the other hand, would prefer the right to strike without the possibility of any compulsory process. That's how the problem arises at least in some areas of the United States.

Bairstow Mr Chairman, when you began the discussion you made reference to the fact that there is a difference in the number of strikes relatively in the private sector compared to the public sector, and that we are seeing an increasing number in the public sector. I have, as you have, noticed the decline proportionately in the private sector. I'm wondering if Jean Boivin agrees that we should take into account a little historical perspective here. Very much of the same kind of turmoil that the public sector is going through now was experienced in the early days of organizing through the dirty thirties and the forties and so on. Are you making too pure a distinction between the kinds of problems that worry the public sector employees, labelling them as public service commission type problems or public service problems, vis-à-vis the labour relations problems in the private sector? These distinctions may be unnecessary because the private sector once had the same problems. Shouldn't we take into account more the problem of the lack of experience of so many new managers in the public service? They are less sophisticated in labour relations problems than are many of the union leaders they bargain with. Some of the union leaders in the public service are specialized and they have had a chance to get into this work gradually. The union people are dealing with managers who for the first time are confronting labour relations problems and simply can't cope. This becomes apparent when analysing some of the issues which escalate into arbitration cases. In arbitration and mediation work, I have noticed some real hostility and antagonisms between the parties that stem from day-to-day job experiences. I believe that we've got a lot of turmoil ahead of us which we could over-legalize by drawing this too fine distinction between the public and private sector problems.

Steinberg The point I was going to make regarding the 'double standard' was covered with care by Professor Aaron. He noted then an irony in the reversal of typical bargaining attitudes, in that California public sector employees opted for arbitration, and their employers for the right to strike, when asked to choose appropriate impasse resolution procedures.

I would add that this role reversal indicates something of the power of economic forces shaping the bargaining process in the public sector. We seem now to be neglecting this factor in our discussions. The comments appear almost unanimously, but perhaps prematurely, to hold that the private sector bargaining model is unsuitable to the public sector. We may in fact have come full circle by overstressing the differences and ignoring the similarities in public and private sector bargaining.

Mitchell I've been closely exposed to both systems when you talk about the double standard – first with the federal government with its very special statutes, and then in the province of Saskatchewan. In Saskatchewan the public service has been bargaining collectively with the government for thirty years without any discrimination between public servants and people in the private sector. In addition, there are no legislative limitations on what is bargainable. It's wide open. Now if you look at the numbers quickly, you would say that it has been a resounding success. In thirty years there hasn't been a service-wide strike. You have a bargaining unit that covers practically the whole service. In thirty years they've had one study session, which was held last fall in support of a cost-of-living claim, and last year in the dead of winter the outside highway workers struck during a blizzard for two days in support of an adjustment in their contract. So it appears to be a success. But, those of us who are closer to the situation know that there are a number of other factors that come into play. We had a trade union that is only beginning to act as a trade union should. It is only beginning to discover that if it doesn't begin asserting itself and reflecting the increase in militancy within the bargaining unit, it is going to be replaced. I think we are going to have some difficult times in late 1975 simply because this trade union must start to show its members that it's in business and that it's a serious organization.

The point that is interesting is that we've had this system for thirty years and because we have that system we can't go to another one. It would be quite impossible for us, politically or from any other point of view, to back up now and say that we would like to have something like Ontario or Manitoba. Once you take these steps they are irreversible. Now if this conference were being held ten or twenty years ago, it would be particularly valuable on this point. We could say to ourselves, and agree with each other that to take the legislative step of putting the framework for collective bargaining in place is a very important step, not to be lightly done, because having done it you can't back up to a more conservative or less progressive piece of legislation.

Crispo Permit me just an observation or two, not in the sense of pretending there's any agreement or consensus because I don't think there is one. I think the real question is: whose double standard? To add to what has been said earlier it seems to me that public employees and their unions want the best of both worlds in two senses. They want it procedurally, which we'll come to later, in the sense that if they're weak they'd like arbitration, while if they're strong they'd like to bring the service to a halt. They would also like a double standard – if you want to put it that way – in terms of the substantive issues: if they are behind the private sector, they want more so as to catch up. Once they catch up they demand more because they claim government should then become a model employer.

I guess I'm still back at where we were on the Task Force when we raised the question of whether there really was a case for separate boards or separate laws for public as distinct from private employers. I doubt that we can get back to that state, if we ever were there, because the vested interests are simply fantastic, not just in terms of the unions having their double standards but in terms of the boards now developing a kind of empire around their public or private sectors. In addition there are some intriguing precedents in our present legal framework. In various jurisdictions we are now treating the construction industry as a thing apart, as we should have for years. I think my bias is still that we should be moving towards one act and one board with a few special provisions and special panels where absolutely necessary.

If the unions are really serious about this double standard let's call their bluff and have a single standard across the board. I'm a little concerned about the way in which they're trying to use this to get what in effect amounts to the best of both worlds. I don't blame them for trying, but I'm not sure I want to bless their effort.

For the moment may I suggest we leave the double standard question. Does anybody want to take up the second issue I suggested which was the so-called catch-up or pattern-following thesis which may help to explain why so many public servants are upset.

Waisglass I would like to start with the 'double standard' question because it relates to the 'catch-up' question. Neither of these factors, in my mind, account for significant differences in the causes of unrest in the public sector as distinct from the private sector. As for most municipal employees, there is no 'double standard' because they are, for the most part, governed by the same legislation as private industry. And as for those municipal employees such as policemen and firemen who in most provinces are denied the right to strike by special legislation governing their dispute procedures, the 'double standard' fails to account for differences in the levels of labour unrest. Compulsory arbitration for policemen and firemen seems to work well in Ontario, but not in Quebec, where the system has been threatened by some major strikes in the past few years.

Consequently, I doubt the validity of the 'double standard' as a significant factor to account for unrest in the public sector. We should search for other causes. This leads me to question the validity of the 'catch-up' argument as a distinguishing cause of unrest in the public sector, affecting it in a distinctly different way than the private sector. To the extent that 'catch-up' is a factor, I doubt if it has been any more important or significant in the public sector.

The large question involving both the public and private sectors at this time is the matter of *relative values and relative incomes* which have become seriously disrupted and generally destabilized with the accelerated inflation rate of the past two years. This, I believe, is the major factor accounting for the rise in the incidence of strikes in both the public and private sectors. We should not underestimate the importance of the display of power in the product markets, its consequences in the extraordinary rise in prices such as for oil and sugar, and the major disruptive shifts in relative prices and relative incomes that have resulted from major shifts in effective market powers. It is inevitable that major changes that disrupt relativities in the pricing system will disrupt relativities in the income distribution system. It is equally inevitable that the demonstration effects of the successful use of power in the product market will have an impact in the labour market. Greater relative power becomes more widely seen and used as a valid means to improve not only relative prices but also relative incomes.

Thus, emulating the demonstrated examples of proven success in the product markets, more and more employee groups in both the public and private sectors have been seeking to strengthen and test their powers to improve their relative income positions, or at least to protect such a position against erosion.

The defence of a relative income position might seem to be a simple question of 'catch-up,' but it is more complex. The higher incidence of strikes in the public sector is essentially the consequences of the need to test, improve, and establish relative bargaining powers. Some public service unions are having their powers tested to maintain the relative income gains made prior to the inflation acceleration, while others are seeking to demonstrate increased relative powers in order to establish an improved relative income position. The power struggle, as I see it, is mainly to establish a new stability in income relativities. The need for the new public service unions to test and establish their strengths in the recent inflation is very much like what the new industrial unions had to do in the post-war inflation. The main differences between 1946 and 1975 are to be found in the nature and character of the new inflation and the new unionism.

In conclusion, I wish to warn against the dangers of seeking single or simple causes of the rise in labour unrest. Obviously the rise in the incidence of strikes is closely related to the rise in the rate of price inflation. But the causes are dynamic and complex. What complicates the current employee struggles to restore, maintain, or improve relative income positions is the related but distinctly different question of status. This, I believe, is the case in the recent strikes of high school teachers in Ontario. Their strikes are much more than an effort to improve their relative income; they are also powerful expressions of their intolerable dissatisfactions with public decisions which downgrade the importance of teachers. I believe the question of status is also involved in many other public sector strikes, such as garbage collectors, hospital workers, and postal employees. They are not only for more money; they are also for the psychological satisfactions the strikers get from the feelings of importance. When they prove the importance of their jobs to the public, strikers win satisfactions that can not be equated with whatever extra income might result from their demonstrated powers. Public indifference or tolerance is the worst thing that could happen to a union on strike. And I do not think there is much difference between the public and private sectors. The most significant difference is that the new public sector unions feel compelled to test and prove their power and importance, which the older private sector unions, for the most part, have established some decades ago.

Thompson My remarks follow from what Harry Waisglass has just said. I think there is a double standard with public sector employees, no matter what the law says, because governments treat public and quasi-public employees differently from the way the private sector treats its workers. Governments make decisions which affect the economic status of their employees for completely non-economic reasons. In the private sector for instance, the relative income or status of a group of employees ultimately is a function of the economic health of the industry or the firm that employs them. That statement is much less true for employees who are dependent upon the government for their income. Governments often make decisions to raise salaries or to increase appropriations because there's an election coming up, or to cut them because of an election and they don't want to raise taxes. Government can be substantially out of phase with the private sector. I think this factor creates enormous pressures within an industrial relation system in the public sector. Public employees see themselves at the mercy of politicians who have goals which may be removed from the welfare of their employees. We have examples in education, for instance, where decisions to lower or not to lower pupil-teacher ratios are made and rescinded on political bases. Incomes policies are enforced first in the public sector. At the provincial level, we have had salary freezes imposed unilaterally on public employees by several governments. In the private sector, radical changes are less likely and more often linked to broad economic change. Such actions by government are an underlying factor which prevades this whole issue, and we shouldn't really blame collective bargaining or unions for reacting in various ways. Labour relations are at the end of a chain of events.

Waisglass Certainly there are differences in goals between employers and employees in the public sector, but there are goal differences also in the private sector. The main difference between government and business organizations is that the latter seek to maximize profits. But both are concerned with efficiency and cost effectiveness, and both have essentially the same conflicts of interests between employers and employees. I do not see how the difference between the public and private sectors, or between profit and non-profit organizations, would make for important differences in the causes of strikes or in the right to strike. Far more important than the differences between the two sectors are the differences within each sector in the causes of labour unrest, the strike propensity of employees, the maturity of collective bargaining relationships, and the public interest factors that might require restrictions on the right to strike.

Jain With regard to catching up with persons in the private sector, many will have to bargain with the provincial government, rather than the administrations of their respective employers. This is what the Canadian Union of Public Employees had to do in Ontario with respect to hospital workers. They realized that the management in general hospitals of Ontario would be unable to come up with a package satisfactory to the needs of their members unless the government increased its funding to the hospitals. Under pressure, the government obliged.

With respect to double standards, administration at McMaster University is in double jeopardy. Although the McMaster Medical Centre is part of the University, the staff salaries such as those of secretaries doing similar work are much higher at the Medical Centre than the rest of the University. This is because the money is coming from two different government departments; in the case of the Medical Centre, the source is the Ministry of Health, while for the rest of the University the financing is through the Ministry of Colleges and Universities. So, the government is acting on the basis of its political priorities; health is up and education is down and hence the double standard.

Another example of double standards can be cited from the United States. In the area of equal employment opportunity, while the federal government was telling private industry that they have to have equal employment opportunity, the government was not providing equal opportunity in the federal civil service. The Federal Civil Service was covered by the EEOA of 1972 for the first time. Similarly, in the area of collective bargaining, the federal government in Ottawa has double standards. While promotions and job classifications are subjects for negotiations according to federal labour law covering the private sector, the Public Service Alliance of Canada is not allowed to negotiate on these issues in the public sector.

Le Bel I think that we must also be prepared to go further when we are discussing the double standard and, even, the 'catching-up' process. We must not forget what Professor Aaron pointed out, that public employees are in many respects very well treated. This is a legacy from the day when these employees did not enjoy collective bargaining rights. Generally, public employers and particularly governments were, despite many failings, concerned to provide fairly for their employees. This was the era of paternalism. Complex administrative machinery, such as Public Service Commissions, were created and legislation was enacted to provide reasonable working conditions for these employees. As a result, they benefited from a remarkable degree of job security and received various fringe benefits which often far exceeded what then existed in the private sector.

Then, came the time when these public employees decided that they were no longer satisfied with the state of affairs and that, particularly on a straight comparability standard, they had been falling behind. However, once the step has been taken from what we might refer to as the paternalistic era into an era of collective bargaining, it may become absurd to retain the major achievements of that paternalistic policy. Otherwise, you have some peculiar situations. For example, a few weeks ago, the Treasury Board was saying that the blue-collar workers in the general labour and trades group could not receive wage increases to bring their wages in line with those prevailing in the private sector since they were receiving various benefits such as the pension plan, which far exceeded what their private sector counterparts were getting. The joke is that these employees apparently did not particularly want the pension plan. Perhaps, if they hadn't been given a chance to bargain over the whole range of their working conditions, these employees might have very well opted to trade away some of their superannuation benefits in order to get a larger wage increase. This is, of course, impossible because, in the Public Service of Canada, the benefits provided by the superannuation plan are not negotiable. Thus, in a sense, collective bargaining may still be hampered by those legacies from the paternalistic era.

We must recognize that this problem of the 'double standard' is not simply one where public employees are receiving less or being given fewer rights than their private sector counterparts. In other respects, they are getting much more because of the protective structure that has been built in long ago.

Once we opt for giving public sector employees collective bargaining rights, these rights cannot be restricted to what, in a paternalistic perspective, might be defined as 'what is good for them.' In many respects, this is exactly what we have been doing up to now. Whereas when a private sector employee is dismissed or laid off, it is considered entirely satisfactory that he has recourse to a grievance and arbitration procedure in which he is represented by his bargaining agent, in the public sector we still retain the rules and regulations and agencies which are designed to ensure that it is practically impossible to dismiss and lay off the public sector employee. Although much criticism is presently directed at collective bargaining in the public service, it could be argued that we are still far from having achieved the transition from paternalism to collective bargaining. Furthermore, these remnants of paternalism are very much resented by the very employees that they are designed to protect. For example, in the Federal Public Service, there are many demands by bargaining agents and the employees that they represent for the right to bargain collectively over the introduction of technological changes; this is not at present permitted because it would interfere with the provisions of the Public Service Employment Act and with the powers given to the Public Service Commission under that statute. These provisions and these powers are really there to protect the employees; yet, they are dissatisfied with these provisions and they wish instead to be allowed to bargain collectively over these issues.

Wilkins Everyone at one time or another finds himself in a 'catch-up' situation, whether it's based on a comparison between public servants and their private sector counterpart or whether it's a comparison between different public servants who bargain at different times. The important point is that for a long time both public servants and the general public have accepted private sector comparability as a fair basis for determining public service salaries. There have to be other criteria as well. And what is important is that such criteria be accepted by everybody, including the public servants and the general public.

It is significant that, in the municipal part of the public sector in particular, there is an absence of criteria. With the possible exception of some cases such as hospital employees, none of the provinces have stated criteria as a guide for dispute resolution for municipal employees. If you talk to private employers, and indeed to some public employers like provincial governments, and ask what level of government gives the greatest competition in terms of pay, the response will usually be the municipal governments. For this reason I take issue with Jean Boivin's point that the municipal public servant is disadvantaged because of the way in which revenue is distributed. My observation would be that the municipal politician by and large is less influenced by the taxpayer's concern for increased taxes than for the taxpayer's concern for disruption of service. Therefore, the municipal politician reacts to the demands of municipal employees more quickly than to the taxpayer's concern. Furthermore, the municipal politician can often pass the buck to the next level of government.

Jean Boivin has made the point in his paper that 'catch-up' problems are exacerbated by the lack of adequate outside references and the lack of timely data. These are problems no doubt, but I don't really think they are in any way insurmountable. Techniques exist to obtain an adequate reading on the market so that public servants could bargain on the basis of a relatively current appreciation of settlements elsewhere. I don't think that the most critical factor is time. More critical is the lack of readily available adequate data and this is a problem that is showing up more and more in studies of the problems in public sector collective bargaining.

Jean Boivin also raised the question of percentage increases pointing out that as long as public service bargaining provides the same percentage increase to all levels, the more populous lower-level groups are going to feel disadvantaged. That's a fair point; but I think it is also important to note that most governments recognize this issue. If you examine the pattern of pay increases, whether bargained or not, management employees tend to get less than those at the lower levels. Unions are recognizing this although rather slowly and a lot of bargained settlements provide for at least fractionally less at higher levels than at lower levels in the bargaining unit. Furthermore, there is increased emphasis on the lump-sum payment for the retroactivity part of a settlement and this in turn compensates the lower-paid employee more than the higher. Also, in the federal government as well as in some provinces, across-the-board cost-of-living increases are usually lump-sum payments that give larger percentage gains to those at the bottom of the salary scale.

A final point is the question of what the public is willing to accept concerning pay for public servants as well as the position of the government as an employer. As unionization increases in the public sector there is a demand for increases which relate to some sort of norm, but not necessarily to precise comparability. Is the public willing to accept that the government be the leader? The government of New Brunswick made a statement in which it said that the government wished to position itself not in the van, not too far in the rear, but somewhere around the middle – and that's a typical government position. It may well be that one of the effects of public service bargaining is that public servants are moving further in the van than they used to be and that this is causing a certain amount of concern on the part of the public generally.

Phillips I want to concentrate on the relationship between the political and market determination of wages. This is illustrated by the recent nurses' dispute in Manitoba. Our premier has decided that inflation is the biggest problem facing Canada and that the unions are asking for too much. The nurses were asking for a substantial increase to bring them into line with other provinces. However, the premier told the hospital boards that they would get sufficient finances to provide for a much smaller increase. The hospital boards were caught in between since they would get less funds than they knew was required for a settlement. In other words, the provincial government was trying to solve the world's inflation problem by restricting the public sector which is, of course, impossible.

The other point I wanted to make concerns the structure of raises. In the last bargaining round with the civil service, the government position was that everyone earning over 1200 dollars a month was to get a lower rate of increase than the lower-paid workers. The problem is that, in many areas in the federal government, professional wages are so out of line on the high side that comparability problems arose. Manitoba civil servants were paid fourteen or fifteen thousand dollars for joint programs with junior federal servants receiving eighteen to twenty thousand dollars.

Peitchinis There are two or three things that I would like to mention and the first one is related to the 'catch-up' issue, which in turn is really related to the whole issue of the change in personal and social values. Workers in the public sector are no longer willing to accept psychic income for being important to the process. Whether they be doctors or nurses or teachers, they have delivered the message that if we regard them as indispensable, then we must pay them accordingly. If we say that teachers and nurses and postmen are so important to the production process in society as to be indispensable, then we must be willing to pay them and to give them advantages that perhaps many workers in the private sector don't have.

The second point, and this relates to the issue of double standards, is that they are no longer willing to accept the fact that they are being legally discriminated against. They appear to be saying that if as citizens we are deprived of certain rights that are legally bestowed on others, such as the right to strike, then a social and political justification must be provided for that decision. This leads back to my first point: they are saying in essence, if you tell us that we should be legally deprived of the right because we are civil servants, then you must pay for that, or you must provide us with some alternative advantages, such as guaranteed employment, higher incomes, better retirement provisions, longer holidays, sabbaticals, or whatever.

There seems to be an incompatability between government as employer and government as legislator negotiating with government employees. It seems to me that this is rather odd: if the government can't get its way in the bargaining process, it can get its way through the legislative process. Somehow these two things should be separated. This is what led me to propose, in relation to collective bargaining on the railways, the introduction of a protective mechanism in the form of an essential services tribunal to engage both in the negotiating process and in the arbitration process from the beginning to the end. Since government is not likely to give up its legislative right, it must give up its negotiative and arbitrative right in relation to its employees. It cannot be both negotiator and legislator.

Carter I'd like to take a run at a sacred cow – the notion of private sector comparability. I think an argument could be made that it represents a double standard because underlying it is the idea that the private sector has to come first and employees in the public sector must follow. However, we now hear public sector employees saying: 'This isn't the way things should be. Our services are just as valuable as the services being performed in the private sector. So why shouldn't we be in the lead?' This is not surprising since in many cases, there are really no viable outside comparisons that can be made. Or if an outside comparison is made, it is based on the value of certain services which are artificially high. One can look at the legal profession, for example, and argue that the value attached to services performed by lawyers are artificially high, and kept artificially high by the type of legal aid program one finds in Ontario where the amount of work can be expanded quite easily. It seems to me that perhaps we should be changing our ideas and perhaps public sector employees should set the pace, being in the vanguard of those receiving wage increases.

Steinberg I very briefly made the point, perhaps too early in the conference, that we were undervaluing the power of economic forces underlying the public sector bargaining process. As we edge toward discussion of Professor Phillips' paper, we seem to be moving toward consideration of economic factors, and in this context let me suggest several loosely related possibilities concerning the present discussion.

First, government employers have discriminated, in the sense just mentioned, because they have often presumed the labour supply curve of government employees to be perfectly elastic. This is in good part because a strong patronage element prevailed in recruitment, and thus a certain paternalism perhaps still remains among some government employers.

Second, it may be that in failing to look hard enough at the impact of economic forces, we fail to see that the 'erratic' behaviour of politicians seemingly out of step with market signals, is no more than a short-run phenomenon. Certainly there are going to be even greater frictions, and therefore lags, in the transmission through the political mechanism of appropriate reactions to economic events in the private sector. Yet we should note that, especially with respect to the labour relations of government employees, the political process is shaped by economic factors. As we will see later, Professor Phillips asserts this as commonplace knowledge early in his paper, but then denies its direct importance. If we fail to assess the power of the market forces reflected in the public sector, we tend to overstate the aloofness and isolation of the politician from these forces, and therefore we tend also to overdraw the intractability of public sector labour relations problems to solution by collective bargaining. I would deny that there are no effective 'costs' to the politician, and suggest instead that the costs haven't been identified and measurement tools not created.

My third point concerns measurement specifically, and may lead us into the area Jaffray Wilkins raised regarding measures of comparability. Professor Carter just expressed concern over the difficulty of finding criteria for wage setting in non-comparable public occupations. Indeed, Professor Boivin noted in his paper that the criterion of comparability with private sector employees could be used as a fetter on the economic progress of public employees. All the more reason for focusing attention on the need to create good measurement norms rather than decry their absence or present uses. So that we may have more guidance even on when to apply comparability criteria, finer measurement is required.

For example, a model might be created that compared first differences in wages for good municipal and private sector counterparts by labour market area in both cross-section and time series. What would be the results? We don't have a good model for Canada as yet, but I'm suggesting that we have a measurement obligation. Jaffray Wilkins has noted that there is a tendency for municipal employees to move toward the median wage level of their private sector counterparts. Without prejudging the issue, I suspect that the Canadian data in such a model as I've suggested would still reveal a differential in favour of the private sector, much as Paul Phillips reported in his paper that Fogel and Lewin had found for the US. I am saying that we have much measurement yet to do before we either throw out the notion or despair of finding suitable comparability criteria.

Crispo I'd like to react to a couple of points, although I'm going to lose on every front the way people are talking. I have had some misgivings about the so-called 'catch-up' issue for over a year now. I think the unions have almost worked it to death at the federal level and in some provinces, and they have gone past it at the municipal level. Their wages and salaries used to be behind, but increasingly they are either even or ahead. At the same time they have greater security – except perhaps for those in academia, where I'm doing my best to get rid of the worst features of tenure. Moreover, at least at the federal level, they have a pension plan that the public doesn't even know is fully indexed. In effect, we've created two classes of citizenry in this country when it comes to pensions: the public service with its fully indexed plan, and the rest of us with non-indexed pension plans.

When you add it all up I really think it's quite debatable whether there generally is a 'catch-up' issue. But what is really significant, and Jean Boivin has borne this out, is the fact that the public service unions are no longer talking 'catch-up,' they're saying: to hell with 'catch-up,' we deserve to be ahead, we're essential. Somebody whose viewpoint on this matter is absolutely appalling suggested we should pay people on the basis of how essential they are, regardless of their skills or anything else. Well, if that's the way we're heading, I've got to get into another occupation because I'm not essential to anybody and I've got to find something else. Maybe I'll take up garbage collection. I've been handing it out for a year, now I'll collect it and get more for it.

I'm old fashioned enough to believe that those who pay taxes and pay for the public services shouldn't have to pay a premium for those who carry out those services. When you allow for job security and better fringe benefits, public servants should get no more or less than comparable groups in the private sectors. If we're going to let public servants lead, knowing the weak-kneed gutless politicians that preside over our governments, we're really going to have runaway wage inflation and nobody will ever put the lid on. So I'm a little disturbed, even if it means jeopardizing my relations with the Public Service

Alliance, the Canadian Union of Public Employees, and the Civil Service Association of Ontario.

NOTES

1 'Avoiding Public Employee Strikes – Lessons from Recent Strike Activity,' *Proceedings* 1970, Spring Meeting, Industrial Relations Research Associations (IRRA), p. 472.
2 'Reflections on the Future of Bargaining in the Public Sector,' *Monthly Labor Review*, US Department of Labor, July 1970, p. 18.
3 *Ibid.*, p. 22.
4 Gus Tyler, *The Labor Revolution*, New York: Viking Press, 1967, pp. 7-8.
5 By public employees, I refer here to all types of employees, whether they are municipal employees, federal or provincial civil servants, teachers, hospital employees, policemen and firemen and employees of Crown agencies. Even if municipal employees do not legally fit this definition since they are covered by general labour legislations in Canada, I think that my considerations also apply to them because many of them are faced with the same problems which are the causes of the actual unrest among other public employees.
6 *Summary of State Policy Regulations for Public Sector Labor Relations*, US Department of Labor, Division of Public Employee Labor Relations, Washington, DC, Feb. 1973.
7 *Melton* v. *City of Atlanta*, Government Employee Relations Report no. 389 E-1, Feb. 1971; *Atkins* v. *City of Charlotte*, GERR no. 286 F-5, March 1969; and *AFCSME* v. *Woodward* 406 F-2d. 137 (8th Cir. 1969).
8 *Summary of State Policy Regulations.*
9 One reason that can possibly explain this substantial difference between the two countries is the fact that the 'local government syndrome' is probably stronger in the United States than in Canada.
10 'Collective Bargaining in the Provincial Public Services,' in *Collective Bargaining in the Public Service*, Institute of Public Administration of Canada, Toronto, 1973, p. 34.
11 I do not pose any value judgment over the objective adequacy or inadequacy of the private sector model for the public sector. I am only stressing the fact that it is a source of concern for public sector employees to be treated in a different way as private sector employees as regards the determination of their working conditions. Such difference between the private and public sectors would be more easily acceptable in Western European countries where there exists a well developed 'sens de l'Etat' among civil servants which is absent in North America.

12 Although in this province, the very wide powers given to the Lieutenant-Governor in Council considerably limit the statutory right to strike.

13 C.A. Edwards, 'The Future of Public Service Unionism,' paper delivered at the annual meeting of the Canadian Industrial Relations Research Institute, Toronto, June 1974, p. 4.

14 *Ibid.*

15 I believe that the same Labour Relations Act should apply to both the private and public sectors but that there should be a separate public sector panel within the regular administrative agency.

16 Accordingly, at least in Quebec, a special legislative intervention during the course of bargaining is usually *not* the final step before the settlement is reached but some kind of intermediate point between the moment when the unions decide to use the strike weapon and that when a final settlement is arrived at.

17 Some people consider this practice as a 'destruction of the normal political process' (Harry H. Wellington and Ralph K. Winter Jr. 'The limits of Collective Bargaining in Public Employment' in *Collective Bargaining in Government*, J. Joseph Loewenberg and Michael H. Moskow eds. Englewood Cliffs, NJ, Prentice Hall, 1972, p. 271). Whether this criticism makes sense or not is out of question once we have accepted the fact that collective bargaining in the public sector has passed the point of no return.

18 Robert D. Helsby, 'A Political System for a Political World,' *Proceedings* 1973 IRRA Spring Meeting, p. 510. Some of these claimants are multinational corporations which receive large subsidies from the governments in order to undertake huge projects which should favour the creation of job opportunities (like the $40 millions received by ITT from the Quebec government). The only difference between these public funds and those which are used to finance the public sector wage bill is that while the determination of the latter is made public, the population has no chance to intervene in the determination of the former.

19 *Ibid.*

PAUL PHILLIPS

Collective bargaining dynamics and the public interest sector: the market and politics

The central question that I have been asked to address myself to in this paper is the comparative dynamics of collective bargaining in the private and public interest sectors with particular attention to an evaluation of the efficacy of the traditional bargaining models and of alternative mechanisms for determining wages and working conditions in the public sector.

First, let me remind participants of the inherent difficulties in such a task – difficulties that I would like to elaborate on not because anybody is likely to be unaware of them, but because they act as critical constraints on the judgments I will be making. It is perhaps unnecessary to begin by stressing that collective bargaining takes place within 'the labour market' and is, indeed, one of the most important institutions through which the labour market operates. But if we are to discuss the dynamics of collective bargaining, we must understand, at least in some general and generally accepted way, the dynamics of the labour market. Unfortunately, one of the first difficulties we face is the state of labour market theory which I would argue is one of considerable disarray. It is unlikely that economists would agree on what 'the labour market' is, let alone how it works.[1]

A second, and related, problem is the political distribution question. Assuming all could agree on the dynamics of the labour market and on the role and importance of collective bargaining in institutionalizing the labour market solution, we have not settled the question of whether this is the outcome that *should* exist. For each and every distribution of income and wealth there is a different market solution. And since collective bargaining is about income determination, the result is indeterminant unless power and value variables are included. This is a vital question in the public sector where, as often as not, there are no market demand criteria. The issues then become by necessity political – what should be.

With these two caveats – first, that the state of our understanding of the workings of the labour market is poor; and second, even if the neoclassical labour market were the prevailing norm, such a market mechanism would not imply that the resulting income distribution is proper or should somehow be applied to the public sector – we can proceed to attempt to define the public sector and/or essential industries, what I have elsewhere called the Public Interest Sector.[2] There is, and can be, no hard and fast definition of the public interest or, more to the point, where the public interest becomes less important than the private interest. Public ownership, operation, or regulation is sometimes used to differentiate but at best it is an imperfect yardstick, if only because governments for reasons of economic development, regional stabilization, civil rights, or other motives, have extended their activities into many sectors of the economy. On the other hand, the private construction industry is not infrequently included in the public interest sector: witness the legislative intervention in the elevator constructors dispute of a few years ago or the recent ironworkers strike in Quebec on the Olympic site.

Nevertheless there are a host of public and private industries, sometimes regulated, sometimes not, where the public has a particular vested interest in any discontinuity in service. In my terms these are 'imbued with special public interest,' being industries which provide direct public services where the general public has an intimate and direct interest in the outcome of a dispute.[3] This definition, I realize, begs the question. But the more one looks at industrial relations in today's economy, the less one can distinguish where 'special public interest' ends and where 'normal private interest' begins. In fact, there exists a continuum of institutional labour markets, some imbued with extreme public interest and, at the other end of the spectrum, those with little public stake. Where one begins and the other ends is a *political* question which, in part, will be determined by the individual case and time.

However, there are seven sectors which are generally considered to have inordinate public interest because interruption of service threatens one or more of life or limb; peace, order and good government; or the basic sinews of the economy. More specifically I would rank the critical industries in the following order:

1. Police and firemen
2. Hospitals and medical care
3. Utilities[4]
4. Transportation
5. Municipal services
6. Civil servants
7. Teachers and educational authorities.

This is a very general ordering and arguments could be made for altering the ranking for specific industries or occupations (e.g., light-house keepers from 6 to 1). One might even question how essential continuity of education services are relative to some industries not enumerated but this is a question I will discuss in greater detail below. What I am inclined to suggest is that the 'public interest' is much more limited or should be considered much more limited than what I suspect might be the general consensus.

Economic loss to those not a direct party to the negotiations is not necessarily a valid criterion. By way of example, the recent strike/lockout of grain handlers, at least in its early stages, should not have been considered as an essential industry requiring immediate public involvement. The fact is that the farmers were not disinterested victims. They were direct parties to the dispute through their agents, the pools and other grain companies. The early involvement of the government ultimately culminating in legislative action was probably unfortunate for longer-term industrial relations. Nevertheless, such action may have been politically unavoidable. This brings me to my optimum definition of the public interest sector. *The public interest sector is whatever the responsible public authority believes it to be at any point in time.* There is no objective criteria. This is not avoiding the question. Industrial relations involves the interaction of political-economic institutions according to rules legislated, interpreted, and refereed by governments who are also significant institutions in the interaction in their own right.

While I have argued that there are no 'pure types,' I do not mean to suggest that there are no significant differences between the extremes of the continuum. Indeed, I have tried to show these differences in a theoretical way in a simple bargaining model.[5] Since the assumptions of the model are important in interpreting the differences between public interest situations and the standard industry situation governed by market criteria, it may be relevant to elaborate somewhat on the basic model. The main assumptions of the standard industry model is that the employer is motivated by the pursuit of profit (or the avoidance of loss) while the union is motivated by the maximum of wage gain subject to the minimization of wage loss to its members through an industrial dispute. Bargaining, therefore, follows a time sequence based on the immediacy of the potential loss or the actual loss occasioned by a work stoppage. The critical assumptions are that the employer is induced to compromise by the economic cost of not compromising and hence precipitating or extending a work stoppage, and that the union is induced to compromise by the economic cost to its members in loss of wages through not accepting the latest company offer. The economic cost to the employer includes loss of potential sales and profit. The cost to the union is the loss of wages to the employees. The latter is a function of the state of the labour market, the availability of alternative income maintenance programs, and the perceived length of the dispute.

I don't wish to repeat all of the argument behind the behaviour of the model but there are important underlying assumptions which bear critically on any discussion of the public interest sector model. Let us first consider the employers expected behaviour. It is assumed that the employer wishes to pay the lowest wage compatible with ensuring the minimum supply of labour for his needs. His minimum 'true' offer, therefore, is constrained by the supply curve of the most scarce occupational group (assuming an occupationally heterogeneous labour force demand and a single bargaining unit). The only inducement to the employer to offer more is the threat that, unless he does, no labour will be forthcoming for the duration of the dispute and the employer will face short-term economic loss (the loss of expected profits and the fixed costs) and possible long-term economic loss through the loss of customary and potential markets, loss of key workers, shutdown and start-up costs, etc. Indeed it may be suggested that the long-term costs to the employer of a labour dispute place far more pressure on a firm to settle than do the immediate costs which, like capital expenditure, can be amortized over a long period.[6] Employers that have a monopoly in the product market and face no long-term loss to competitors obviously stand to lose much less, a factor that will (other things being equal) reduce his willingness to compromise.

The maximum a firm can pay is presumably determined by *long-term* profitability which includes consideration of the course of future prices and productivity rather than the specific price, productivity, and demand at the moment. This alone would tend to produce a higher maximum for firms in concentrated industries, because market power permits greater upward price potential, and for capital intensive industries with high productivity gain potential and a low ratio of wage costs to total costs.

The course of the offer curve over time is much less easy to hypothesize because it represents reaction behaviour. The employer's reaction depends on how he perceives the power and will of the union. This is only on part determined by the state of the labour market. It is also determined by the skill of the union leadership, the militancy of the union membership, working conditions, availability of strike pay or other income maintenance, and the knowledge, skill, and approach of the employer. A chippy employer who resents unionization and attempts to undermine the union in his operation is likely to offer less than an employer who accepts unionization and wants to develop good and stable relations with the union. Furthermore, industries seem to have traditions that have a substantial influence on particular bargaining patterns, from the conciliatory type of low initial demand, high initial offer, and gradual compromise type of bargaining in some industries (such as would appear to be the case in the printing industry in Manitoba) to what might be described as 'brinkmanship' (such as characterizes the forest industry in BC). Nevertheless, the general pattern of offers can be argued to follow the pictured path.

On the union side quite different constraints operate. The maximum a union will initially demand is in large part determined by the 'tradition' as described above but this is often merely grandstanding. The true first demand is usually constrained by the union's estimation of the firm's ability to pay as modified by the 'going rate of wage increase,' current rates of inflation, and considerations of equity and the response of public opinion. The minimum is constrained primarily by what the members will accept rather than bear the costs of strike action. This is heavily influenced by 'going rates' in the labour market, but a comparison of union rates for similar occupations in different contracts is ample evidence that comparability is hardly determinate.[7] Thus the union minimum is much less determinate in terms of market criteria than the employers' maximum. Alternatively, we can say that the minimum is much more political and therefore subject to considerably greater uncertainty. Indeed, we must admit that it can hardly be really described as a true minimum. Yet we have sufficient cases where a union has preferred to see an employer close down or hire strikebreakers and resume operations rather than concede to a lower settlement. In such cases, there are obviously operative minimums.

The course of demands over time are subject to similar influences as affect employers' behaviour; that is the perception of the employers' power and will. Once again this perception is a function of a large number of factors in addition to strict labour market and product market conditions. However, once again we have suggested a general pattern.

Having summarized the bargaining model for the private interest sector, we can now turn to the question of what happens when we change our assumptions about the constraints that act on the parties to conform to what might reasonably be assumed about the constraints and pressures in the public interest sector. *The absolutely critical assumption in our system of collective bargaining is that contract agreement is reached because of the economic loss or potential of loss to both parties occasioned by a work stoppage.* Without the potential of loss, the system breaks down completely.[8]

While I have argued above that there is continuity in the spectrum from extreme private interest to extreme public interest, there are strong reasons to distinguish within the public interest sector between essential or emergency industries and those imbued with special public interest because of ownership or because of their central importance to the entire economy or polity due to their infrastructure or utility role. The former have to be considered as different because of the immediacy and irrevocability, particularly in respect to human life, of the costs of a dispute. The latter have to be considered as different from the industrial norm because of the magnitude of the costs, primarily in economic terms, of a dispute. In general, therefore, it makes more sense to make a distinction between essential industries and 'other' industries than to distinguish between the public interest sector and the private interest sector. In any case, the justification for public intervention to prevent work stoppages or to circumscribe or end stoppages rests on quite different grounds.

Before discussing the nature of the costs of the dispute which is essential to the previous argument, it is necessary to elaborate somewhat on the nature of the 'public' and 'private' sector and the market/

non-market distinction. The constraints in our industrial model presented above operate only when the employer is producing for a market. Firm ownership is, of course, not the relevant criterion. A privately owned transit system, defence equipment manufacturer, or doctors' clinic operating under medicare are not usually producing for the market in the generally accepted sense. In contrast, many publicly owned firms do produce for a market, albeit in many cases a regulated one. One hesitates to attempt to define the limits of the market and those of the non-market distribution system. Yet it is probably necessary in order to understand the contemporary industrial relations dilemma. A brief diversion is, I think, warranted.

The most illustrative approach is an historical one. Our industrial relations system had its origins in the second half of the nineteenth century and has borrowed heavily from Great Britain, the spiritual and empirical home of economic *laissez-faire*. Much of our legislative and legal concepts of contemporary collective bargaining are descendent from what the Webbs defined as the 'liberal' period.[9] The conception of industrial relations is of the bilateral monopoly type described in my model; that is, a private employer producing for (and constrained by) the market, negotiating with a union supplied (and constrained) by the labour market.

The reality of the post-Keynesian, neo-capitalistic world of the period since the Second World War, however, is one where the non-market sector has become very significant – some might even argue dominant. The political process has determined that an increasing percentage of national output shall be distributed through non-market mechanisms resulting in the universal availability of 'free' goods and services. For purposes of this paper, this process is neither good nor bad – it simply exists. Assuming this trend continues, and there is no reason to suggest that it will not, the question of public sector bargaining becomes of increasing concern in our mixed capitalist type of economy as government expenditure continues to rise in absolute, if not relative, terms. In short, the private-sector industrial model elaborated above is becoming increasingly less relevant for the following reasons:

a. the employer maximum is negated by the existence of oligopoly market power and the acceptance of the reality that governments will not accept mass unemployment and hence will increase demand through monetary and fiscal policy thereby creating price increases which lower real wages (as Keynes suggested) and, in turn erode the effective ceiling constraints on wage offers by employers in concentrated industries;

b. the growth of the non-market and regulated sectors tends to blur, if not extinguish, the suggested market constraints;

c. the increasing capital intensity and specialization in the labour market masks, or at best weakens, the labour market constraints;

d. the increasing size of firms and their interrelations tends to increase the impact of a work stoppage.

In short, the problem is getting bigger, the answer more elusive.

To consider the effect of these trends on our standard model let us first consider the employer position. We can identify four positions on the spectrum: the emergency service employer (public or private); the critical commodity or service producer (defined in economic terms); the important commodity or service producer; and the marginally important employer. These classifications must be defined in terms of two variables – the immediacy of the impact and the magnitude of the impact. The general term of 'public interest' does not distinguish. For example, the strike of firemen in a small town may bring an immediate and catastrophic local impact, but in national terms the magnitude is small. Alternatively, a strike of grain handlers may have limited immediate effects but, if sustained, may produce huge economic consequences for the nation. Suffice it is to say that we have no market criteria to define what is and what is not critical to the public interest.

This leads to the general question of the differences in bargaining between the public and private sectors. The above should indicate that the relevant dichotomy is not the simple public-private one. Rather the model can be used to explore a different classification of industries.

Essential-emergency industries

The model illustrates that the dynamics of 'essential' industries produces an immediate impact on the labour market. Assuming that the workers and the union face no extraordinary pressures, the model implies that the cost to society is so large and so irreparable that there is no realistic 'market solution.' The result is a crisis solution.

Before one jumps from this conclusion to a defence of the arbitration solution, let me point out that the latter is equally unsatisfactory. If one assumes that the workers have no right to strike, then the employer need not raise his offer. It is true that legislation may provide that a third party be appointed to adjudicate. Assuming the best intentions in the world, the result may or may not approximate a market solution since there is likely to be no objective indicator of the market for occupations in the essential-emergency occupations – there being no jobs in the private sector that quite approximate the essential-emergency jobs.[10]

The attribute of essential-emergency industries that sets them apart from others and makes work stoppages intolerable politically is the immediacy and irrevocability of potential results. Since we can't value human life or limb in marginal productivity terms, the market model fails. But in our system when the market standard fails we have nothing in its stead. The ultimate determination, therefore, must be through the political process.

Utilities and controlled industries
These types of industries differ only in degree of immediacy from the foregoing. Obviously, an interruption of electric power in the grip of a prairie winter differs only marginally from an interruption of emergency services. The major difference is that there may be a greater degree of comparability on the labour side of the market with the industrial model. Still, the economic effect possesses a degree of immediacy that is not handled by our model. In addition to the immediacy and irrevocability, the magnitude of economic loss is also very likely to be large.

To be more systematic, let us review the forces operating on the two parties in a bargaining situation. It is true that the employer in a utility may face economic loss in the short run. But utilities and regulated industries by their very nature tend to be monopolies so that there is much less danger of long-term losses and, in any case, the demand curves they face are very inelastic so that price increases to regain losses are more feasible. In other words, long-term profitability does not constrain the employer to anything like the same extent as our standard model employer. On the other hand, these types of monopolists also often exhibit elements of monopsony which tend to increase their bargaining power in the labour market.

To the extent that these employers are regulated monopolies, therefore, ability to pay becomes a much weakened constraint, and if the firm is monopsonistic then comparability – 'just' increases – is greatly weakened. In short, we tend to have bilateral monopoly, largely unconstrained on the employer side by economic criteria. The union faces the same pressure from its members to settle to prevent the disruption of their incomes, but these same members are likely to have very different conceptions of the employer's resistance. Obviously, Ontario Hydro is not going to close down.

In bilateral monopoly, theory does not tell us what the ultimate solution will be. This is determined by power relationships. But since power is exerted through a disruption of service this means the loss of the utility which has no alternative supplier, at least in the short run and for most uses in the long run as well. Because of the immediacy and magnitude of the losses occasioned by the interruption of service, there is an almost inevitable invitation to intervention by the political authority. Such an intervention becomes an ingredient in the bargaining strategies of both employer and union and once again economic criteria give way to political criteria.

Transportation and transit

Transportation services are, in some senses, the most interesting of all public interest sector cases. Interruption of services usually involves no immediate threat to life and limb. But transportation is the critical element of infrastructure in our modern economy such that a strike or lockout threatens the vital sinews of the national, regional, or local economy. The degree of immediacy of economic impact varies as does the over-all magnitude. The critical point in our analysis, however, is that the cost elements to the two parties in our model in no way reflect the total social costs. All transportation *systems* exhibit to some degree monopoly power. From the employers' side, loss of customers is only rarely a major long-run cost. The widespread subsidization of some modes of transportation, particularly transit systems, greatly reduces the impact of short-run losses.

It is true that comparability with the market sector may be more feasible providing that the comparable market solution is deemed to be just. But since the public sector is so heavily involved and may even dominate the labour demand side of the market, and since the externalities are so significant such that identifiable marginal productivity is not a very reliable measure of social product, then the external market may not be considered a relevant standard.

Nevertheless, given the intense pressures on the general economy that result from a dispute in such a basic infrastructure industry there develops intense political pressure to force a settlement. If one needs empirical verification of this, one need only recollect parliamentary action in the rail strikes of recent years. Unfortunately such legislative action appears to constrain only one party to the dispute, the workers, particularly since in most cases the legislative authority is directly or indirectly the employer.[11]

Civic and Crown employees
As a group, municipal, provincial, and federal employees present diverse characteristics, some of them considered above. The majority, however, may be deemed to fit into a classification that, should a labour dispute occur, occasion no immediately observable or irreparable loss to the general community. It is true that the inconvenience of the interruption of assumed services can be quite visible, as with the withdrawal of garbage collection, and indeed threatening, as in the case of a walkout of snow removal personnel in central Canada in mid-winter. But, like the mills of the gods, most of the processes of government grind slowly and a cessation of their motion has its impact in more indirect ways.

Nevertheless, the winding down of critical governmental infrastructure and decision-making bureaus which, despite the popular criticisms, are essential to the functioning of the modern polity and economy, must eventually begin to exact a heavy economic and social toll. By way of simple example, dispute-occasioned delays in the city planning process can delay major development projects tying up large amounts of costly capital. The problem is that the groups in society who bear the costs are not, in the normal sense of the word, parties to the dispute and may not even be aware that they are ultimately the losers. Indeed, governments that take hard lines with their employees' unions often parade as public beneficiaries, saving tax dollars and 'holding the line against inflationary wage demands.' This is most noticeably the case if the government concerned has proclaimed a policy of fiscal restraint as implied in wage-price guidelines and similar pronouncements. At the extreme, governments can appear to gain monetarily since considerable expenditures are saved while tax revenues are in large part uninterrupted. In this respect, the government is the atypical employer whose revenues are not greatly reduced by a labour dispute.

In terms of our model, therefore, the market determination of the employer acceptance path is replaced by a politically determined path which is, it is true, influenced by economic loss – but economic loss to third parties whose effect is felt through political pressure on legislators. To further confuse the issue, provincial and federal governments have the legal right to legislate the termination of a strike, within the limits of civil disobedience, on their own terms. In practice, governments may turn over to presumably independent third parties the task of recommending or imposing settlements. But this raises the familiar problems of comparability, justice, and credibility that plague all interest arbitration situations.

Teachers and educational authorities
Finally, I would classify teachers, other educators, and support staffs in a separate category. They are obviously essential to the economy and society in the long run, but in general the threat to the economy or to the life of the student arising from a strike or lockout is initially minimal. Such may not be the case, of course, if the dispute is protracted over many months, but that is largely true of any dispute in a major industry, such as a pulp mill in a single-industry town. I suspect that much of the political concern that accompanies a teachers' strike is occasioned by two factors: the personal inconvenience of working parents and of all other parents who must make provision for bored children in the home; and second, by a continuing, possibly subconscious, belief in the empty vessel theory of education which would suggest that if a child misses 10 per cent of the school year, some 10 per cent of the child's brain will forever remain empty.

It is fortunate in many ways that both teachers and school boards seem to accept the social mission of education since it appears to promote compromise in an industry where there are few market standards on either side of the table and, at least as far as teachers are concerned, virtually perfect degrees of monopoly and monopsony. One other reality is that school taxes are generally independent of a dispute whereas education expenditures are not. Labour demands, however, are ultimately only constrained by the prevailing antipathy to 'death and taxes' that affects all public negotiations.

Sovereignty, legitimacy, and comparability
In the preceeding sections, I have tried to illustrate what I consider the important variables in public-interest sector industrial disputes and to define the difference between essential industries and public sector industries. The distinguishing characteristics are immediacy and irrevocability on one hand and total economic and social impact on the other. As to the latter, the duration of a dispute becomes a major factor in the designation.

No discussion of public sector industrial relations would be complete without some reference to the sovereignty issue. In simple terms,
it can be argued that governments cannot accede to industrial action
because to do so would compromise the sovereign authority to govern
conferred on the legislative body by the will of the people expressed
through the ballot box.[12] Such a doctrine, however, has become an
anachronism in an age when governments have become the largest
single employer in the economy and where the labour markets in
which governments operate are structured so that no competitive
norm exists.[13]

But I don't think that one can dismiss this issue quite so simply as
of no import. Governments are elected to govern with all that this entails in terms of fiscal responsibility and responsibility for the aggre-
gate performance of the economy. As we know from Quebec's experience with the United Front, governments are loth to turn over to
third parties wage determination in the public sector because of the
sheer magnitude of the possible consequences for the public treasury.
Also, as British experience has dictated, collective bargaining may be
incompatible with an incomes policy which, after all, was the legislative creation of the elected body. The government as policy-maker,
therefore, may well conflict with the government as employer in so
far as 'free collective bargaining' is concerned.

This must lead to some discussion of alternatives to the traditional
industrial bargaining model. Without going through all the arguments
about the right to withdraw ones' labour as a basic human right, we
can separate alternatives into two classifications – alternative mechanism of dispute settlement within a conventional collective bargaining
framework; and replacement of the collective bargaining system with
some other mechanism for determining wages and working conditions
for public interest sector employees. Modification of the collective
bargaining process includes the 'arsenal of weapons,' the most popular
being some form of compulsory arbitration as a final solution to impasse. I am not impressed with arbitration as a general solution to the
problem despite the fact that it may appear to work in some cases.[14]
Even then, I would argue that arbitration only works in the longer
run if both parties believe that the results are reasonable. This in turn
means that the governmental body cannot intervene to influence the
award. Thus sovereignty in fiscal and economic policy matters is no
more protected under arbitration procedures than under collective
bargaining. On the other hand, the threat of a strike or lockout of

essential services is eliminated – providing, of course, that the workers accept the legitimacy of the procedure and the justice of the award and do not resort to wildcat walkouts, mass resignations or work-to-rules.

The question of illegal strikes in the public sector tends to make much of the foregoing discussion somewhat academic. As our survey of strike activity in the public interest sector revealed, one third of the stoppages were illegal or wildcat.[15] To some extent this reflects the particularly legalistic format of the North American industrial relations system. But it should also underline the potential futility of seeking purely legislative solutions to the problem. In short, any alternative to, or restriction on, the standard model must have a legitimacy that is accepted by the rank and file. One such basis of legitimacy is the acceptance of comparability with private sector agreements. Nevertheless, there are problems with comparability both at the practical and at the conceptual level.

Let us first consider the practical difficulties.[16] The most obvious is the difficulty in determining comparability. At one extreme, there is no market occupation quite comparable to that of the police constable or even of the nurse.[17] At the other extreme, say maintenance tradesmen in the civil service, ostensibly comparisons are more feasible. But even in this case difficulties arise as soon as one attempts to apply the system. Civil servants presumably have greater job security. How then does one modify for the potential loss to the industrially employed through unemployment? Private sector employees can bargain about working conditions and pensions, issues which are often excluded from the bargaining table for public employees. Is this worth anything? Promotion potential may vary. Should this be taken into account? Indeed, can it be taken into account? Which employer is comparable since wages for the same occupation vary widely firm to firm? Is there, as there appears to be, a trade-off between wage levels and turnover such that a firm may pay high wages as an incentive to lower turnover rates while another firm will absorb the higher costs of turnover by paying low wages? If this is the case, which strategy should the government pursue? Should comparability be with all firms, only unionized firms, only firms over a given size? Should comparability apply occupation by occupation or, in the case of occupationally heterogeneous bargaining units, only to percentage increases over time?

Further, what geographical area is to be the basis of comparison?

In the case of federal employees, justice would seem to dictate that all employees in the same occupation be paid the same wage. But this would seem to run afoul of regional standards of comparability. This is a particularly difficult problem as illustrated by the strikes of airport firemen in Vancouver last year. Similar less drastic variation occurs within provinces, most often on a rural-urban basis.

One last complication is the difference in the availability of overtime which in many occupations is a major attraction because of the multiple rates earned. The consequence of regular overtime is a higher average hourly wage and often some discretion over hours of work and, thereby, take-home pay.

These practical problems of comparability are difficult enough, but there are conceptual difficulties as well. By this I mean that acceptance of the market standard, however perfect or imperfect it may be in theory or in practice, is to accept the principle of no policy intervention in the determination and structure of wages even though wage payments constitute the dominant portion of all factor payments. This precludes any form of government incomes policy, narrowly or broadly defined.[18] This, of course, is as much or greater a threat to 'sovereignty' as union action in the public sector because, strictly adhered to, wage rates in the public sector would not reflect any public control on either side of the market but would reflect only the decisions of employers and workers and/or unions if organized, in the private sector. Such a solution, even in a conventional economic sense, can only be considered equitable if all labour markets are competitive and in simultaneous equilibrium.[19]

Let me also raise further theoretical objections. Let us assume an occupation where the public interest sector at a point in time employs a significant proportion of the labour force in a particular occupation. Thus, although the supply of labour may be homogeneous, the demand for labour is not. Let us further assume that, in the private sector the marginal revenue product is low because private demand is limited by income constraints of the general public. On the other hand, the marginal social revenue product (due to externalities) may be very high. However, if the wage is determined by the private sector market, an insufficient supply of this type of labour will be available to the public sector. Thus we will have the familiar case that the political authorities refer to as a shortage of this specific occupation. Therefore, if we apply the strict comparability standard, this means that the public sector is precluded from using wages to attract more labour to meet politically determined social needs.

One possible solution to this dilemma is for the public employer to raise its occupational wage until its needs are met. But these needs are politically determined by budget allocation and administrative decision so that no market criteria can hold. To further complicate the situation one must ask the question: within which time frame? If we assume that the elasticity of labour supply increases with time, then the so-called equilibrium wage will depend on the politically determined rate at which new hirings are desired. It will also depend on the level and occupational structure of unemployment.

Further, we can consider the problems raised by the existence of internal labour markets.[20] The existence of an internal labour market severely limits the determination of market wages at all but entry occupation levels. However, the questions already raised should be sufficient, both on the practical and theoretical level, to challenge the basic presumption of determining public-interest sector wages by comparability to the private sector market. It should also be noted that the problems increase as public sector employment rises relative to the rest of the economy, that is, as public goods and services increase in proportion to private goods and services – a trend that appears inevitable in an increasingly complex and interrelated economy characterized by a high income elasticity for public goods and services.

A significant shift has been occurring in the underlying supply and demand conditions in the labour market. Public education has massively increased the supply of white-collar workers, particularly given the sustained increase in female participation rates. The social status of these occupations has thereby been diminished at the same time that unionism and technology has improved the conditions and raised the wages of blue-collar and private sector jobs. At the same time social security systems and Keynesian economic policies have greatly reduced the insecurities of private sector employment. As a result, the perceived comparative advantage of employment in the public interest sector has declined and this has been a significant long-term factor in the demand for public service unionism.

I think that one can gather from this that I am not enamoured of any fiat or arbitration system for determining wages and working conditions in any sector, in theory or in practice. At the same time, I admit to having no alternative simple solution. Nevertheless, the basic presumption upon which I believe a successful industrial relations system must be based in our contemporary kind of society is not that justice must be done (since we have not agreed upon a definition of distributive justice) but that a rough justice must be perceived to have been done in the view of the participants. Given the prevailing ideological norm, it seems to me that collective bargaining as practised in most of the private industry sector at present is, in the common view, the closest approximation to that datum. What then of the public interest sector?

First, I have already argued that the distinction should be made between essential and public interest sectors. The former is characterized by the immediacy and irrevocability of the costs, the latter by the magnitude of the costs to the general public over the longer run. Because of the importance of this distinction, the two should be treated separately.[21]

Public-interest sector disputes should, for the most part, be treated like private sector disputes through collective bargaining leading to the right to strike or some form of voluntary arbitration. In the case of impasse, the decision to enforce an end to a dispute is a political decision which should be taken by the appropriate political body through *ad hoc* legislative action. The effect of such a procedure is to introduce considerable uncertainty into negotiations thereby tending to encourage settlement along lines suggested by our basic industrial model. Nothing, of course, can protect us from bad legislation, although recent experience in Britain would indicate that justice was not seen by the electorate to have been done to the miners with the resulting defeat of Mr Heath's government. I would argue, therefore, that this indicates that the system worked. I would also tend to argue that it eventually worked in British Columbia although in a different context. The failure of the Social Credit government to permit free collective bargaining in the teachers' case led to organized political opposition by the BC Teachers' Federation which, presumably, was a factor in the change in governments.

Some may regret this politicization of collective bargaining. I think, however, that it is inevitable and that it therefore should be open and the merits of the case argued in public. Only the vigilance of the opposition and the media, however, can restrain the vested interests of a government legislating in its own behalf.

Essential or emergency industry disputes cannot be treated in quite the same way. Speed of settlement is essential because of the immediacy and irrevocability of the costs on the public. All sorts of alternatives have been proposed or are in operation, from wage determination by government fiat, through compulsory arbitration to the right to strike subject to certain limitations such as the maintaining of designated services, and even to the legally unconstrained right to strike. As indicated above, my preference is for a system that maintains the essential elements of the industrial model. How can this be achieved without disastrous and politically unacceptable disruption of services?

In the model, compromise leading to settlement is induced by economic costs to both parties through the loss of wages to the worker and loss of business to employers. While the former holds in emergency disputes, the latter has no relevant meaning. Perhaps the same can be approximated by some form of statutory strike. For example, assume that firemen and a city reach an impasse. On the declaration of a strike, essential fire protection services would be maintained by law but the firemen would not receive any wages. The city, by law, would be required to pay into a fund 150 per cent of the pre-strike wage bill, funds which must not be recoverable. Thus both sides would have the economic incentive to reach an agreement without the threat of disaster. Such a system, of course, does not guarantee justice or freedom from illegal wildcat walkouts, but it does come closer to approximating the standard industrial practice that, with all its weaknesses and problems, we still accept as the least of all evils.

DISCUSSION

Crispo Thank you, Paul. I wonder if we could endeavour to organize our discussions around the various points you've raised. I picked up six areas. One was the degree of essentiality of the service. The second point you raised was the degree to which the disputes in the public service are bound to be politicized. You also made a major issue of comparability which we discussed earlier but which some of us may want to explore further. I was also intrigued by the emphasis which you placed on female militancy. You obviously feel that this underscores a great deal of union militancy especially in the public service. I wasn't as conscious of that being a major causal factor of our current difficulties, but I think it's worth discussing. In addition, of course, you hit on the conflicting roles of government as employer and as guardian of the economy. Finally, you went out on a limb when you suggested we should perhaps – and I noticed you used the word perhaps – experiment with statutory strikes. So there's a lot of food for thought in your paper.

Bairstow One of the points which was mentioned by Paul Phillips that I find the hardest to deal with in any reference to government service withdrawals is that 'the public won't stand for it.' That statement was made about a particular kind of strike. How do you assume 'the public won't stand for it'? It is obvious that in certain localities the public tolerates certain kinds of strikes; in others they don't accept strikes such as firemen's strikes. Can you be so certain about the public's reactions?

Phillips Perhaps I should say that the politicians believe that the public won't stand for public interest strikes.

Bairstow I keep thinking about that recent firemen's strike in Montreal. It lasted far longer than anyone would have predicted in terms of public tolerance of a strike of that kind.

Crispo One of the things that Canada has proved over the past three to five years is in just how many sectors we can now take strikes where we thought we couldn't possibly take them before. I'm not in the business of congratulating politicians these days – I despair of them – but one thing I would congratulate them for is the amount of restraint they've shown in the face of strikes which ten years ago the public would have thought of as being intolerable and the politicians would have been forced to move on. Quebec is exhibit A. Everybody strikes there, and while I hate to say anything kind about Bourassa, his record is almost as good as Trudeau's for saying 'ho-hum, it'll work itself out, let's not panic.' And by and large things have worked themselves out without undue public hardship.

This country, more than most others, has learned to take strikes in sectors where it was unthinkable for strikes to occur ten years ago. And so I'd like to supplement Frances Bairstow's question by saying that the public is learning to take it.

Phillips For a few days, even for a few weeks, you can have a firemen's strike. But wait until you get an inferno during one of those strikes. I remember the Saskatchewan doctor's strike in 1960, when guns were being toted because of the fears. Now as it happened, the death rate fell during that strike.

Carrothers Sick people moved to neighbouring provinces!

Phillips The fact of the matter is that the government caved in partly because of fear. Even if we could have lasted six months without the doctors, the destruction of the social fabric makes the cost too high.

Aaron I just wanted to add a footnote that I think supports one of the points Professor Phillips was making; that is, the importance of the public perception of strikes by public employees. In the State of California there is a bill pending that provides for a very limited and carefully circumscribed right to strike. Now the opposition to that provision, which I think is eventually going to be dropped from the bill, is coming from the public at large. Citizens are inundating the legislators with mail threatening them with the worst kinds of retaliation at the polls if they vote for this legislation with its right to strike. Public management has made a 180-degree turn from its position of a few years ago and is now saying that it favours the right to strike and no compulsory process whatsoever. Organized labour is also for the right to strike. It is the legislators in the state government who are going to defeat the strike provision, if it is defeated, solely because they can't stand the heat from the citizens who are writing to them. Now we've had public strikes in California, even by firefighters and police, and the foundation stones of the Republic are still standing. Nothing serious really happened, and that is what persuaded public managers that they can really do better with the right to strike than they can with some group of fact-finders or arbitrators telling them what they have to do by way of resolving the dispute. But to the general public, the thought that any public employees can strike is so appalling that legislators who support such a right are being threatened with defeat at the polls.

Johnston I suspect that Canadian public opinion is probably fairly similar to that of public opinion in California. On the one hand, we've had any number of teachers strikes, some of them of considerable duration, where the public didn't rise up in arms. On the other hand it's obvious that the government has been agonizing for almost two years, over whether or not to give the *legal* right to strike. The reasons for agonizing is that they believe their constituents are not yet ready to give teachers the right to strike as a matter of principle, even though they're tolerating it as a matter of fact.

Crispo Just to supplement that point for those of you who don't know: the situation in Ontario is absolutely fascinating right now. Both the teachers and the school trustees have come out for the right to strike. I have reason to believe that even the government wants to give them the right to strike. But the caucus of the Conservative party in this province is balking at this notion because the backwoods are weary about it. But to turn to another subject, I would like someone to explain why Canadian politicians have resisted and really put up with more public service strikes than their US counterpart, despite what appears to be an equally hostile public opinion.

Woods I can't give you the answer, but I agree largely with what Paul Phillips said. I've been impressed with the degree of tolerance of the public towards public service strikes. There's an incredible degree of such tolerance in Quebec at least. Only in two situations was the public really upset and that was with the police strike and the firemen's strike. We had learned that the damage from strikes in public service occupations is relatively less than we had thought it was before they took place. We've also learned that segregating police and firemen for special policy treatment was sound if the Montreal experience means anything. We had sixteen bank robberies the afternoon that the police strike started and violence and vandalism accompanied the firemen's strike.

The Manitoba Government Employees Association which bargains for all civil servants in one global agreement, in 1969, got the government to agree to take away their right to strike, in return for arbitration. They were granted a statutory right to arbitration and a statutory prohibition of the strike at their own request. At the same time the representative of the management committee bargaining for the government was insisting the MGEA must have the right to strike and they should not have the right to arbitration. But there's been a change. Last summer an arbitrator in the government employees case rendered an unpopular award and the militants in the government employees association increased in numbers and the majority of them now are demanding the right to strike. They had formerly told the Manitoba Labour-Management Review Committee there was no point in them having the right to strike. They could not use it, because they bargained in this one global unit and there were not enough militants in the organization to support a strike. But now that militancy has increased because of an unsatisfactory arbitration board, attitudes have changed and they are demanding the strike right. Where the public stands on these issues, I don't know.

The joint committee operated for two years in the examination of this public sector labour relations problem, and we invited a number of public sector employees and public sector employers to sit with us. At the first meeting one representative from the hospital association said we should ask the government to take away the right to strike from all government employees. He didn't get support from anybody. Throughout the whole two years emphasis was on making collective bargaining work rather than on the right to strike and there was no pressure for the strike prohibition at all from the parties of interest.

Crispo Could I just ask, you say the public has grown more tolerant of public strikes?

Woods No, I think they're getting less tolerant, but I think over the years they've been remarkably tolerant.

Crispo But the polls are frightening to me because over the last few years there has been a rising proportion saying that they have had enough of both public service and essential service disputes. Yet, contrary to the experience in the United States, to a fairly large degree – and wisely so – our politicians are saying, 'I'm sorry we have to live with this, it's a free society.

Arthurs I'd like to venture three practical reasons for governments not yielding to this public opinion in Canada. The first relates to our political culture. It's much more difficult to take reprisals without 'reprising' a government on many fronts. The whole notion of the parliamentary system is that you can't vote out individual legislators without voting out the whole party and that's quite difficult to do. It's quite difficult to mount a one-issue campaign which will effectively displace the government.

Second, I think that governments appreciate the radical difference between outlawing and stopping strikes. Governments are not anxious to be put in the position of trying to stop something they have out-lawed if they cannot effectively do so.

The third point, and one that I think is really important, is that so long as the dispute is to be settled by a rational process of arbitration, spending priorities are handed over by the government to somebody else, to the arbitrator. Now that may happen *de facto* in a collective bargaining situation, but at least the government isn't put in a position of defending its spending priorities and submitting them to a rational, articulated review by an outside person. It's a practical matter. They can hide money in different parts of the budget, and plead inability to pay or do a number of other things that they would be very loth to do in terms of an arbitrated settlement.

Johnston There's a question that comes to my mind as to whether public intolerance works to the advantage of the employer or the employees. I'm beginning to think that it now works to the advantage of the employees. The public doesn't like the strike and as a result it forces the government to settle at a higher rate. I think there is some evidence of this in Ontario, where the public servants threaten an illegal strike and the government settled at something like 23 per cent.

Bairstow One of the factors that had to be taken into account is that it is fallacious just to consider the money objectives which lead to a strike. There are other advantages that accrue after a strike as a result of concerted action on the part of the employees. If you look at what the Public Service Alliance group got in the last negotiations and strike, 4 per cent doesn't seem like much for a strike effort. But to the union, the 4 per cent is not everything. They may have accomplished some of their other objectives of educating the members as to how to carry out a strike. The strength or power this demonstrates to the public may be worth far more than the monetary gain. I think we should be careful in thinking only in terms of the monetary results.

There is another factor in the Public Service Alliance situation that just can't be analysed scientifically. For years the Alliance people have been talking publicly about going the strike route. They have been restless and have been testing themselves and I believe they have to get it out of their system. Now whether this means they will want more strikes, or be able to tolerate more strikes, I don't know. But they did learn a lot about strike strategy which they may want to apply the next time.

It may well be that by resisting the original demand and achieving a settlement within a certain figure, the government may have exemplified the economic limits of their policy. These limits may apply as well to subsequent labour disputes which are known to be in the offing. One can't judge this yet, but one could argue that in such a case the strike works to the advantage of the government. However, it is very hard to identify this as a policy.

Waisglass From the ideas expressed here, I think there is some consensus that government interventions to restrict the right to strike should generally be avoided, and that it is not practical or possible to predetermine all of the exceptional situations that would require such intervention. The main determining factor is the degree of public tolerance of a strike, and this is something political leaders can influence. For example, a few years ago, the Trudeau government had a measure of influence in raising the level of tolerance of a postal strike. In addition, there would be a higher degree of public tolerance for hospital strikes in Metro Toronto if only one hospital is on strike at any one time, rather than all being on strike at the same time. Timing is another important factor. The strike of plough operators in Saskatchewan, mentioned earlier by Bob Mitchell, had a public impact, because there was snow on the ground; they would not have the same impact in the summer. Similarly, strikes in grain storage and transportation have had a greater impact in the economic circumstances of the past two years.

Paul Phillips presents the concept of degrees of essentiality. Conceptually, there is no problem. The ideas are sound, clearly expressed and acceptable. I would question, however, its application to his ranking of critical industries. One reason is that the essentiality of some industries has not yet been strike-tested. For instance, he does not consider the banking industry to be critical, probably because its employees have yet to organize and prove they are 'the sinews of the economy' and have a great public impact, even if they are not classified in the public sector. Furthermore, there might be some measure of error in equating the essential and critical nature of an industry with that of its employees. Because the banking industry had the power to maintain, or even improve, its relative income position does not mean that its employees have equivalent powers. More dramatically, because the fuel oil industry had the muscle to substantially improve its relative prices and incomes does not mean that its employees have the same capabilities.

In essence, therefore, the essentiality of an industry is an important consideration, but it is not sufficient to determine public policy decisions on restrictions to the right to strike. What is more important is relative bargaining power, which, in Neil Chamberlain's terms, is the capacity of one party to raise for its opponents the costs of not settling on its terms, in relation to the cost of settling. In both the public and private sectors, there are some unions that have sufficient bargaining power to raise their relative incomes more than other unions. The public reaction, or its intolerance of a strike as an excessive or injurious use of power, is not always predictable. It is in the political process, rather than the economic process, that the point of public intolerance is determined to restrict or curb a particular strike.

Why, then, is the public authority usually so prone to resist interventions? Mainly, because such interventions really say to the strikers that they have proven their importance and power and that this entails an economic price. Whether the public can resist or tolerate a longer strike could determine its outcome in relative power and income positions. Another reason for the reluctance to intervene is the value we place on freedoms and the rights to self-determination.

On the question of why the incident of strikes rises with accelerated inflation, the kind of inflation we have had recently has exposed the effectiveness of brutal and naked power in redistributing incomes. Established and accepted relativities in prices and incomes have been disrupted. The pricing and income system is in disarray. It is under such conditions that established criteria of comparability are questioned, tested, and possibly changed. Also, in such conditions, relative bargaining powers are more likely to be challenged and tested. Comparability criteria can remain fairly stable only in periods of relatively stable prices, when most price and wage changes do not vary greatly from the average price and wage changes. In periods of price instability, when many prices increase much more than the average, comparability criteria are corroded. Any sense of order in the pricing system is quickly lost, and with it any sense of fairness, reasonableness, or equity that might be ascribed to price changes. The disarray in the product markets is soon transmitted to the labour markets. Those with the greatest bargaining power get the greatest improvements in their relative incomes. To prove its bargaining power a union would take strike action, although a strike threat might prove sufficient. The assertion of power serves not only to obtain a better settlement at the moment, but more important, to obtain more favourable criteria to be applied in future contract negotiations for maintaining a better relative income position.

This explains the greater propensity to strike during this period of accelerated inflation. It also explains what John Crispo mentioned, that we now have many new public service unions which had not previously been called upon or had not been subjected to pressures to test their bargaining powers, and to establish more favourable criteria of comparability. Thus, inflationary conditions encourage new unions to prove their bargaining powers and old unions to re-affirm their vitality.

Phillips I agree with you. The distinction is not the one we usually employ, between what we call the public sector and the private sector. The whole point of my paper is that this is not the correct distinction. Almost any industry – banks, construction – can be in the public interest sector depending on the individual situation. And I agree with the comment about hospitals. If hospitals strike one at a time there is no economic problem. There is very little cost to the government because there is no major inconvenience to the public. In other words a crisis has to be created in this situation in order to get administrators to settle. But once this occurs a strike becomes politically intolerable.

It is true that you can be as tolerant as you want of a firemen's strike or a hydro strike, but if they cause one death, you'll have a single issue that will affect an election, as indeed the British government found out when they were caught in the miner's strike. There is a point at which the economic and political problem is such that it will poison the situation for years to come. I don't think that there is any simple solution. There is a line at which the bargaining models don't work, and where they don't work there's nothing we can do to make them work.

Stanley After having realized the problem is that we're dealing with a public interest sector, and that there aren't any economic costs that can be calculated on either side, doesn't the challenge then become to attempt to define what the public interest is and develop some system of applying the public interest considerations in such a way as to resolve the dispute rather than to come up with some way of introducing economic costs into the system? I take it you are as serious about this as it appears in the paper. It seems to me that after having defined the problem at the beginning, the idea of introducing economic costs into the system really isn't the solution.

Carter When you get into the public sector it's very difficult to measure bargaining power in economic terms. Unions are beginning to realize that their real bargaining power is in their political impact. The more noise they make, the greater the public intolerance and the greater the likelihood of government intervention.

At one time I thought that large bargaining units could provide stability for the system, making the strike unthinkable. First of all, you couldn't get all the employees out on strike, nor would the public tolerate such a strike. Now I'm beginning to change my opinion. I think it's quite possible to get a large bargaining unit out on strike by raising the expectations of the employees. For example, in Ontario the Civil Service Association demands something in the neighbourhood of 65 per cent. Obviously, they were attempting to raise the level of militancy of their members and, by so doing, they were persuading their members to strike as a group. Now I'm not convinced that such a large unit would have gone on strike, but I think the government believed it and as a result the employees got a very favourable settlement.

Perhaps this means that collective bargaining is the wrong way to treat this type of problem. And perhaps we're fooling ourselves when we say that a collective bargaining structure would depoliticize the matter. Depoliticizing may not be possible because bargaining power is now measured in political rather than economic terms. Should we come to grips with that reality and treat it simply as a political problem?

Crispo What do you mean by treating it as a political problem? Governments are known to buy votes; should they now buy their employees?

Carter Perhaps we shouldn't pay such adherence to the collective bargaining model. Perhaps we should look for other solutions. I know this is probably heresy within this group because we all have a vested interest in collective bargaining, but is it the way to solve this problem?

Le Bel You seem to imply that raising the expectations of groups of employees to the point of militancy is somehow unusual or abnormal. Yet isn't this what collective bargaining is all about? Such a development is at the core of the collective bargaining process and yet you seem to suggest that it is a new development particular to the public sector, and almost an unfortunate one.

Carter I don't think it's new. It's probably new to the public sector and I think, of course, it has the effect of making the strike much more influential or perhaps even making a strike possible. Perhaps five years ago a public sector strike was an impossibility. Now it's a possibility and I think it's being used for political purposes.

Steinberg Don Carter has been saying that the politicalization of public sector collective bargaining makes it distinct from the private sector process, and therefore perhaps an inappropriate vehicle for labour dispute settlement. He suggests that we might possibly want to search for an alternative. I would strongly agree with Professor Phillips' opening statement that 'hard-nosed' legislation as such an alternative tends to be ineffective in solving public sector labour relations problems.

However, much of the burden of Don's argument, and that of others today, has fallen on the non-comparability of the public and private sectors, and on the apparent inability to devise tools for measurement of comparability. At the risk of burdening you with repetition of my previous statements, I am not overly persuaded by the difficulties.

Professor Aaron's paper describes some exceptionally creative, and at least in the short run, successful efforts to establish criteria and measure comparability. Further, the measurement problems Professor Phillips raises in his paper are the very ones that journeymen, government, and public sector union negotiators face daily across the bargaining tables. They are always confronted with issues of non-comparability to which answers are constantly required and for which *ad hoc* measures are continually created. If labour peace is a reasonable measure of success in solving the problem of non-comparability, are we then arguing that public sector labour relations are less peaceful than private sector relationships? For example, after accounting for the difference in proportion of workers organized, and shorter length of time collective bargaining has been available in the public sector, are we saying that proportionately fewer public sector negotiations are resolved peacefully than private sector ones? I suspect not, though I haven't explored that possibility. If, on the other hand, we argue that public sector negotiations are more critical to the public weal, whatever the proportion of labour strife, then we are back to measuring injury to the public weal. Does the strike of marriage bureau clerks seriously damage the morals of the nation? Is their strike more or less destructive to the common good than the strike of garbage collectors? We really need to attempt all sorts of measures of the 'unmeasurable.'

The point I really want to make goes back to the question of bargaining power and begins, again, with Professor Phillips' paper. One of his opening statements supporting the argument that the private sector bargaining model is inappropriate to the public sector is that labour market theory is in a state of disarray. I quickly agree. Queue theory and the radical dual labour market theory challenges to the neo-classical concept of the labour market are unresolved. But, because we can't quite agree on exactly how the labour market may operate doesn't mean that any labour economist would seriously argue that underlying market forces are inoperative. Nor does Professor Phillips say so. Yet, while he spends the first part of his paper arguing that these forces are so buffered as to be inoperative in the public and essential services sectors, he concludes in his last two pages that he had no alternative to offer but a modified private sector bargaining model. I agree as completely with his conclusions as I disagree with the weight he has given to much of his argument.

At this point I run the risk of being the deserving butt of the old Economics 100 truism: teach a parrot to say 'supply and demand,' and you've got an economist. Nevertheless, undaunted, I argue that all of us would agree *ceteris paribus* that when the supply of workers in a particular occupation increases, a downward pressure of wages is generated for that occupation. Similarly, if demand for that occupation increases, there emerges an upward pressure on the price of that kind of labour, and this is true whether the movement actually occurs or is only implicit because frictions have kept those movements from taking place. I think we would all agree that this is precisely the answer to the wage discrimination practised against Professor Phillips' office workers. The supply of these workers has, for a variety of social and technical reasons, shifted to the right and pushed the price of their labour downward. A somewhat longer term and perhaps more sophisticated example suggests that the impact of Sputnik eventually so enormously increased the supply of college graduates and their teachers that the supply schedules shifted to the right, and a long-term market clearing process is now in effect. Not only are college-trained people hunting and taking lower paying and less prestigious jobs than anticipated, but the price of their labour is being pressed down despite institutional ratchet effects that tend to limit the erosion of real as opposed to money wages.

Having delivered this unsolicited Economics 100 lecture, what is my point? I think we are overstating the buffering of economic forces in the public sector. Moreover, with respect to Professor Phillips' second argument, we may be misinterpreting the lack of market cost on the public employer to mean that there is no effective cost constraint in the public sector. In this sense I think we are overstressing the notion that increases in the public budget are easy to pass on to the public under the pressure of government employee wage demands. We are implying, to coin a concept, that the wage-taxes elasticity of demand for public employee services is unity – that any proportional increase in the government wage bill will automatically elicit a proportionate increase in tax yields by government fiat.

Under such an assumption, if as feared, bargaining power alone determined the government employee wage rate, we would be suggesting that the theoretical wage rate could vary from zero to infinity, and its precise determination is entirely a function of the relative bargaining power of the adversaries. Put this way we would all acknowledge that the notion is foolish. There must be an upper limit even if we have not yet identified its parameters. Since the lower limit is unequivocally the supply curve for labour, I would argue that we need to identify more carefully the upper limiting mechanism that seems very effectively to replace the market cost constraint. Were there not an upper limit to the bargaining range and the 'wage-taxes elasticity of government labour demand' were indeed unity, there would be little struggle over public servants' wages except for political window-dressing, and certainly few strikes. Instead, experience points to a bargaining range even in the public sector, and something very similar to the bilateral monopoly model as a good explanatory device in which the determinate wage solution depends on the relative skill and strength of the bargainers. Until the upper limit constraints are better understood and measured, perhaps in marginal social cost terms, we should not so blandly assume there are no effective upper limit cost constraints.

The more essential the service the higher the marginal social cost is likely to be and the more reason we should try to use our ingenuity in devising measures and criteria that would have general acceptance in the political context. This measurement process is in fact evolving through experience in public sector and essential services bargaining. The degree to which we perceive their essentiality will influence both their marginal social cost, and be influenced by distortions of labour supply, and thus influence wage differentials.

Crispo You're going to come up with a mighty odd wage structure. As an economist you ought to be ashamed of yourself! You are going to have an uneconomic wage structure that neither allocates labour properly nor clears the market.

Steinberg Nonsense. The rate for a pipe welder in Fort MacMurray is far greater than that for a pipe welder in a Halifax Dockyard, and both tend to be market-determined.

We are all assuming something about the effect of strikes on the strikers that few students of labour relations would agree to. We imply that the experience of striking makes the litigant strike-prone. Yet experience seems to indicate that the weight of responsibility for and during the strike is a very powerful deterrent to would-be strikers. Unless there is a pathological element in the situation, the strike tends to be a sobering process. Consider in perspective the very question that Harry Waisglass raised regarding the postal workers. As soon as federal bargaining rights were granted, and the cabinet announced a 'hands-off' policy, a wide-open bargaining situation existed and was allowed to run its course. Hard attitudes on both sides resulted in a nation-wide strike that lasted three weeks or more in which no ordinary mail moved in the entire country. Some years have passed since that strike during which time critical issues have arisen in the postal service that were theoretically far more difficult to cope with than the initial problems that sparked the strike yet there has not been another nation-wide shutdown of postal services. There has been a good deal of nastiness and some rotating strikes and work-to-rule attitudes, but never since have the employers created the environment, or the workers undertaken, to close down the whole national service. I'm suggesting that both sides learned something from the initial strike experience. This initial strike experience doesn't guarantee immunity from nation-wide strikes in the postal service, but it seemed to help.

Thompson I'm pleased to see that there is such a consensus that bargaining in the kinds of industries we're talking about is essentially political. The real thrust of Paul Phillips' paper was that he's taking economic concepts – intellectual tools if you will – and applying them to political realities. Costs can be treated in a political sense just as in economics. Furthermore, there is a nexus between politics and economics. After all, what impels politicians to feel that the cost of a strike is so high that they have to do something? Aside from industries vital to safety, the answer to that question is usually economic. Certainly this has been the case in transportation in Vancouver, where costs to prairie grain farmers are involved in longshore strikes.

But the main thought I want to leave is that we really haven't tried to ascertain the economic costs of labour disputes. We all see that this strike is costing x million dollars a day, knowing these estimates tend to be unreliable and often false. For academics interested in these problems a very fruitful line of thought and research is to examine the issue of costs so that when a politician asks if the cost is getting high, the response can be something other than a public opinion poll or a visceral reaction. If one looks at inflation, there is at least a standard of comparison in OECD figures. Maybe we should try ascertaining possible standards for labour disputes.

Christie I want to start by making, in a simpler way probably, an earlier point. It seems to me an essential fact which we all recognize is that in the private sector the impetus on the employer to settle is economic hurt; a hurt which the employer usually feels quite directly. In the case of a large corporation the decision-makers may feel the hurt somewhat less directly but, nevertheless, there is a good transmission process.

In the public sector we are talking not only, and in some strikes not even primarily, about economic harm. We are talking about 'people harm;' the way in which people are hurt and the way this is transmitted into the public decision-making process. In other words, the fact that the public managers do not know and cannot measure the total economic cost of strikes in their sector is only part of the information gap. There is also a non-economic cost to ordinary people, many of whom are powerless because they are unorganized and probably inarticulate; and that cost is even more difficult to monitor.

I share the general assumption here that we have passed the point where there should be any question of abandoning the use of collective bargaining in the public sector, but I think we delude ourselves if we fail to recognize that there are still a great many people in this country who make no such assumption. Certainly, in the relatively conservative corner of the country where I live, there are many who question the propriety of a system of settling the wages of part of the population on the basis of a test of how much the population in general can stand in terms of being deprived of things they think basic to the life that they are used to living. Let me say first that perhaps they have a point. Perhaps we should pause to question the appropriateness, or the morality if you like, of settling public economic issues by means which put pressure on people who do not have any real part in the decision-making process. Second, I suggest that those of us who believe in collective bargaining and think it can be made to work in the public sector delude ourselves if we think that the public is simply developing a tolerance for the inconveniences they suffer.

In my corner of the country I perceive that there has been a continuous build-up of resentment, at least since the Public Service Staff Relations Act came into effect, and that this resentment is furthered every time private individuals are hurt in their day-to-day lives. There is an increasing number of people who have been directly hurt in their personal lives in a way they are not going to forget – such that I fear that if it were to be made a big election issue five years in the future the public sector collective bargaining 'baby' might get thrown out with the right to strike 'bathwater.'

The question of the economic hurt to prairie grain farmers is a real and serious one, but there is also by now a considerable accumulation of people who are seriously inconvenienced rather than economically hurt. They are also unorganized and inarticulate, but they *are* voters and they do not forget.

Crispo What you are stressing, and I would agree, is the very real danger of a public backlash. The cumulative effect of these strikes start to get to people. If this builds up, some political party will make it an election issue.

Johnston The frustrating thing about this whole discussion is characteristic of the whole dilemma of trying to come to grips with public interest disputes. Here we all sit in this room, and I say this kindly, all but four or five of us mainly from academic backgrounds, dealing with this matter mainly as an intellectual problem. I don't think we are too effective for the obvious reason that it is a political problem, and on top of it being a political problem it is a fairly emotional problem. The four papers all seem to come to the same conclusion in one area: keep the process flexible and don't outlaw things in advance since it's better to deal with the problems afterwards on an *ad hoc* basis, when public pressure has jelled. Although we probably all agree with this conclusion, there remains the problem of translating it into legislative and political terms.

For example, it seems as though everybody agrees that we might as well give teachers the right to strike since they have got it anyway. But a few members of the legislature, including some cabinet ministers, don't believe this to be what the public wants at this point in time. So if you think it's difficult to sell the school board and teachers and everybody else in favour of the right to strike, how are you going to sell the idea that hospital workers should have the right to strike, even though their situation isn't much different. It looks as though they'll do it even if we tell them not to.

Perhaps the way to translate the right to strike into political reality is to somehow find a means of educating the public more on this whole subject, and then focusing that public opinion in a way that the politicians can read it accurately. It seems that politicians have not read public opinion accurately at the moment since they apparently read it in one way in an actual strike situation and in another way when they're talking about it in generalities.

The only attempt to come to grips with this question is the idea of the Public Interest Disputes Commission. We've got all the authors of that assembled here today and I hope that we'll hear something about what was good about that idea, perhaps something about why it didn't apply at the time, and perhaps whether it has any chance of applying now.

Goldenberg I think there is a very great gap between what is theoretically desirable and what is practically realizable. That is why I must disagree with the concept of the statutory strike. It may be great in theory but I can't see it working in practice. It assumes a degree of rationality and sophistication that certainly seems to be absent in the public sector. It also ignores the psychic satisfaction of the strike that was mentioned earlier.

I can't help but comment on the reference to the postal strike, particularly to the fact that the postal workers were taken as an example of public service employees who had their one great nation-wide strike and got it out of their system. If the postal workers don't strike, it's not because they are riding on the psychological satisfaction of the last strike. It's damned expensive to carry out a nationwide strike. Having done it once or twice already, they may now find that their strike fund will only take a rotating strike. That's my reading of the situation. Anyway, the uncertainty of a rotating strike has almost as much of a paralysing effect on postal services as a general strike. This is why Jake Finkelman recommended that a lockout be permitted in the face of this kind of thing.

Adams Just two points and they are addressed to Professor Phillips. The purport of his paper – and I think the purport of the entire discussion – is that the private sector is a model to emulate and thus the principal task is to accommodate the public sector to a private model. However, one really has to ask the economist whether a private sector exists any longer. I would suggest that the private sector is not a model that we should emulate; that the private sector doesn't exist; and that there has to be a great deal more public accountability in the so-called private sector because of its public impact. The private sector has a tremendous impact on all of us and it is often an irresponsible sector in this regard. Thus by our saying we want the public sector to emulate an irresponsible sector we get into a kind of double bind. Accordingly, I think we really ought to be very serious about the kind of new solutions and procedures that have to be imposed on the private sector while simultaneously taking off 'the wraps' in the public sector. I would suggest that more concern must be given to the forms of public dispute resolutions, be they fact-finding, mediation, or other procedures mentioned here today.

The other observation that I wanted to make – and it relates to what we've all talked about this afternoon – is about public tolerance. Public tolerance worries me, as it does others, but for a different reason. When we look to the private sector and we say that the private sector is to be emulated, we are referring to mature collective bargaining relationships in the private sector and we have in mind some of the classic compromises that have been made in the private sector. We are impressed by their problem-solving and then tend to assume that everyone can do this. But the public sector is an inexperienced sector at collective bargaining. And my fears are that it's going to continue to be immature because of public tolerance. I don't know what you do about this – whether the public can be educated is of critical concern. However, the public may never let the bargaining process take its course. In any event, the bargaining process can't take its course in the public sector the way it has in the private sector so as to enable the maturity and the co-operation that has taken place in certain private sector contexts.

Take for example the steel industry, where a few years ago it was decided to opt for a form of voluntary arbitration. Terrific co-operation! Why? Because the entire system was threatened by foreign competition. And so it was decided this was the only way the industry could keep the empire, 'a joint empire.' In the public sector this can't happen; there is no competitor, unless it's really an apocalyptic choice and then wage and price control will be the order of the day. Thus, my fear is that we will never achieve mature collective bargaining in the public sector because bargaining can't run its course to cause the kind of maturity that the private sector has stumbled upon in many instances.

Woods First, I'd like to make an observation about Shirley Goldenberg's comment on the statutory strike. I agree that it is not practical, particularly in the public sector. Even if you could take away some of the public revenues it doesn't hurt the people on the employer side who are handling the strike. One of my students suggested a modification of the statutory strike for public employees, namely that the money you take from the public authority should be taken from the salaries of management rather than from general revenues; that might speed things up.

On the remarks of George Adams, I agreed with everything he said except that I would not be quite as pessimistic as he is about public tolerance of the strike. But I agree with him that I think we've got to search for new things. I don't know quite what they are but I suspect, picking up his theme, that we've got to engender a lot more bargaining by the parties in the public sector, and possibly even the private sector, over their own procedures as distinct from their dispute settlement efforts. Perhaps it's necessary to get the employers and their unions in the public sector together and remind them that they are confronted by a hostile public that wants them to solve their union-management problems without harm to the general public.

Goldenberg I don't see how this is possible if, as the case of Quebec last time, one of the parties takes as its motto 'casser le système,' –

'down with the system, down with the other side.' If it's not just 'down with the government as employer,' but 'down with the whole political system,' then you have a different ball game. At the federal level I could see a dialogue of this kind where real collective bargaining is taking place. It is quite possible that we may have real collective bargaining again in Quebec, but as long as the two parties are diametrically opposed in a political sense, I think it is difficult to sit down and work out mechanisms.

Crispo That's a little bit like dragging out the communist issue. Everybody looks for the communist who is causing all the trouble. If you simply say that collective bargaining can't work because a 'common front' is out to destroy the system, I think you are overstating the importance of the employees' political association. Don't forget that they represent a lot of people who are not politicized at all and they can only go so far with that kind of program.

Waisglass The question is this: for those who are looking for alternatives to strikes, are we looking for alternative ways of demonstrating, testing, and changing the relative bargaining powers of the contending parties; or are we looking for alternatives to bargaining power as a means to get a more equitable distribution of income? And if we are looking for substitutes for power or muscle in determining wages and salaries, why then are we looking for something that is really very greatly different from the way prices are determined in the product markets? Why do we have so much less tolerance for the use of power in the labour markets than in the product markets, and why does the public seem to have less tolerance for the role of power in determining labour incomes than other incomes? I suspect it is mainly that a union's use of its powers has much greater visibility.

Phillips In my paper I did introduce the statutory strike suggestion with great scepticism, although I suggest it really hasn't been looked at much in terms of the public sector. It has been looked at and experimented with in the US, primarily in the private sector. Some claim that it has had great success.

On the question of comparability criteria in public and private sector bargaining, it is possible to develop comparability criteria only if true bargaining exists in the public sector; not if it's done by a pay board and by decree as is common with civil services. You cannot negotiate comparability when one side unilaterally decides. Maybe the thing to do is to bargain over what is comparable and then, having decided what is comparable, the rest would follow. In fact, this is what happened at Manitoba Hydro where they agreed to apply the average wage rates of the top firms to hydro workers. This procedure broke down last time, but perhaps the principle of accepting comparability could work.

On the casual factors of strikes, I agree basically with Harry Waisglass that inflation always causes strikes. If you go back in Canadian history, every period of inflation has been accompanied by massive strikes, particularly in the public sector. The Winnipeg general strike, for example, followed a period of declining real wages associated with rates of inflation approximately the same as what they are today. If inflation persists, so will unrest and strikes. Inflation is the causal factor.

The final point I would like to make is that the rules of the economy are changing and we can't look to the private sector for the answers. The fact of the matter is that, in all western industrialized countries, the government sector has expanded relative to the total economy. Since services have a higher income elasticity of demand than goods, and since technological change is more feasible in goods production than service production, then the trend is to an even larger government sector. In addition, the size of firms in the private sector is increasing. Consequently, a nation-wide strike in any major goods-producing industry gets the same demands for intervention as in the public sector. Thus although the growth of the public sector implies some public sector problems in the future, it will be unfeasible to look to a dwindling private sector for the answers.

Crispo What worries me most is the feeling that somehow this new system in the public service has become obsolete before it has been given a chance to work. I don't think that view is widely shared here, but it may be. I hope you'll forgive me one small comment about the federal jurisdiction which is the one I think that is troubling everybody. The Public Service Staff Relations Act is not working in a manner to ensure a fair test of collective bargaining in the federal public service. This is because it's a loaded and impossible system, with the strong increasingly prone to strike while the weak go to some lunatic arbitrator who gives them as much as the strong. Moreover, how can you call it collective bargaining when the government has granted its employees the right to strike but doesn't have the right to lock out? As a result the unions can kill us with rotating strikes as the postal service has shown. Furthermore, there is some doubt whether the government can even lay off postal workers when there's no work to do. The postal unions are going to challenge the government under the law and argue that when the carriers turned up and no mail was sorted because the sorters were out on strike then the carriers should have been paid anyway.

Now when you get that kind of asinine legislation on the books there is an almost hopeless imbalance of power. At the very least there should be lay-off and lockout provisions in the act. In addition, unbelievable fragmentation of the bargaining units exists in the public service. Just look at the airports and airlines where you have to phone to see if they are in operation. There are approximately a dozen groups that could shut down the Toronto airport, and that is madness. The airports and airlines represent a good case in point of why separate legislation is crazy because some of the unions are under one Act and the majority are under another Act. And nobody can straighten out the mess by joint bargaining or anything else. In other words, no one board could begin to introduce any semblance of sanity in that field.

In connection with the post office, why don't they pass a law that makes private mail service legal? Do you know that in the United States the parcel post portion of the public post office has been lost to a private enterprise that's doing a better job than the post office ever did. Competition would put our post office under in short order. This notion that Paul Phillips has that we should let that octopus in Ottawa grow forever and smother us all is a dreadful one. We should dismantle some part of that place up there and the post office would be as good a place as any to start.

I won't write off the concept of collective bargaining in the public service because I don't think it's really been tried. It's very one-sided, unbalanced and unfair from the point of view of the employer. And until we put it in proper shape, let's not write it off.

NOTES

1 For an interesting comparative assessment of labour market theories, see David M. Gordon, *Theories of Poverty and Underemployment*, D.C. Heath; Toronto, 1972.

2 Paul Phillips, 'Theoretical Problems of Public Interest Sector Industrial Relations,' appendix to the *Report of the Manitoba Labour Management Review Committee on Public Sector Employee-Employer Relations in Manitoba*, July 1974, p. 1.

3 *Ibid.*

4 Usually Crown corporations or regulated private corporations.

5 Phillips, 'Theoretical Problems.'

6 The amortization period, of course, is much longer than the contract period. This results from the fact that the negotiated increase becomes the base for the following contract negotiation. Similarly, the workers' amortization period is subject to the same considerations operating, in their case, to reduce the weight of the immediate cost in lost income.

7 While unionization is significantly related to wage variance in specific occupations according to studies now underway at the Manitoba Economic Development Advisory Board, it explains only a small part of the total variance.

8 The most turbulent and violent periods of labour history have occurred when the employers have had access to military, police, government or judiciary powers to prevent or limit the right to strike. Likewise, strike insurance tends to greatly undermine the constructive value of a strike in promoting settlement through compromise by the employer.

9 For the Webb's historically based classification system see S. and B. Webb, *Industrial Democracy*, London, Longmans, Green, 1917.

10 It may be argued that there is an inherent bias in the arbitration system. Most frequently, arbiters are professional men, as often as not lawyers. Being professionals in the higher income classes and personal associates of businessmen and business legal representatives, one suspects a class bias in interest arbitration.

11 I have argued this point in 'Are We Being Railroaded into Arbitration?' *Labour Gazette* 1974. The railroads receive operating subsidies which are not unrelated to their labour costs.

12 This argument can also be countered by reference to the ability of the courts to constrain the government from doing specific things even those popularly backed by an electoral majority (e.g., Bennett's 'New Deal' legislation in the 1930s). Thus, governments do not have unconstrained sovereignty, nor have they ever had it. Nor would I think that many would want the government to have unlimited sovereignty in our pluralist political system.

13 Some studies would indicate that public sector wages do differ significantly from private sector structures. See for instance Stephen N. Perloff, 'Comparing Municipal Salaries with Industry and Federal Pay,' *Monthly Labor Review*, Oct. 1971; and Walter Fogel and David Lewin, 'Wage Determination in the Public Sector,' *Industrial and Labor Relations Review*, April 1974.

14 M. Thompson and J. Cairnes, 'Compulsory Arbitration: The Case of British Columbia Teachers,' *Industrial and Labor Relations Review*, Oct. 1973.

15 Paul Phillips, 'Collective Bargaining Practice in the Public Interest Sector in Canada,' appendix to the *Report of the Manitoba Labour Management Review Committee*, p. 18.

16 Note a similar list of practical and theoretical difficulties in comparability in Fogel and Lewin, Wage Determination in the Public Sector,' pp. 411-14.

17 It may be argued that there are private nurses. But it is obvious that the employment situation is so dominated by the public employers that the market is meaningless. The situation is comparable with the dominant firm price leadership case where fringe firms exist but have no independent effect on the price which may be marginally lower or higher depending on local conditions than those of the dominant firm.

18 Fogel and Lewin, 'Wage Determination ... ,' p. 416, conclude that public employers are more generous in jobs where the private employers' wage 'is relatively low because of monopsony or highly elastic supplies of unskilled laborers who are relatively immobile.' Yet such a policy may indeed be a good social policy.

19 This would imply continuous full employment and instantaneous market adjustment. Since no one would argue that either exist, the question is whether the reality is sufficiently approximated by the theory. This is a question of judgment, but I would argue that it is not.

20 See Peter Doeringer and Michael Piore, *Internal Labor Markets and Manpower Analysis*, D.C. Heath, Lexington, Mass., 1971.

21 It should be noted that it is conceivable that some industries might fit at various times into either of these categories. Hydro is a case in point. In midwinter on the prairies, hydro becomes a life and death necessity very quickly. This is not generally true in midsummer.

JAMES G. MATKIN

Government intervention in labour disputes in British Columbia

Listening to the general public on the subject of public interest strikes leaves one with the impression that there is a crisis of confidence in the present collective bargaining system. While much has already been written on the subject of public interest disputes,[1] after reading this literature one is struck by the credibility gap that exists between the experts who do not seem very concerned and defend the viability of the existing system, and the general public who are intolerant of and fed up with strikes and who call for alternatives such as compulsory arbitration and labour courts.

From the perspective of government, the issue of intervention is a matter of degree, measured not only by the objective, proven harm of strikes, but also by the subjective willingness of the public to tolerate the effect of labour-management disputes.[2] 'A general desire to keep government intervention to the minimum,' said Chamberlain and Schillings,' does not permit keeping it at less than the minimum which is publicly acceptable.'[3]

The law has been the major instrument through which government intervenes to protect the public interest from the threat of strikes. In the Province of British Columbia, the law has been altered dramatically during the last seven years by government attempts to deal with the problem of strikes in essential services.

We have gone through two contrasting periods in British Columbia – from 1968 to 1972 under the Mediation Commission Act (MCA)[4] by which a permanent, predictable solution emphasizing compulsion prevailed, to the subsequent repeal[5] of the MCA after 1972, to the use of the new Labour Code of BC since 1973[6] in which the emphasis is now on *ad hoc* pluralistic solutions based on voluntarism.

I propose to review our experience in BC during these two periods in order to compare the merits of government intervention with the merits of government restraint. At the outset, I must confess to a bias in favour of legislative restraint for, philosophically, I subscribe to the perspective of Oxford's Professor Otto Kahn-Freund, who warns: 'Altogether, the longer one ponders the problem of industrial disputes, the more sceptical one gets as regards the effectiveness of the law. Industrial conflict is often a symptom rather than a disease. I think we lawyers would do well to be modest in our claims to be able to provide cures.'[7]

In my view, experience in British Columbia during these past seven years has proved the wisdom of Kahn-Freund's advice. Ironically, based on our experience, a case may be made for the proposition that legislative restraint will indeed solve more labour disputes in the public interest than will legislative intervention.

To begin with the interventionist period of the ill-fated MCA, it will be pertinent to identify some of the historical forces that influenced this piece of legislation, because it may be true that the basic concept behind it was never properly tested owing to the circumstances accompanying its introduction, and other external factors.

The crucial historical force was the relationship between the trade union movement in British Columbia and the Social Crédit government in power at that time. The animosity and ill-will that separated these two bodies had been building up over a period of many years and was reflected in the province's labour legislation. For example, the introduction of the MCA was preceded, in 1959, by what some persons have considered to be the most restrictive picketing legislation on the continent.[8]

Although an adversary relationship between labour and government is common, and can even be healthy, I believe that, prior to 1968, the problem went further in British Columbia; it had a pernicious side. It would not be exaggerating to say that, in those times, many trade union leaders – and, in particular, the leader of the BC Federation of Labour – believed that the government of British Columbia was the enemy of labour.

The manner in which the bill was first introduced in the legislature illustrates the deep distrust that existed between labour and government. Without warning, the Federation's head, Ray Haynes, was summoned to Victoria by the Minister of Labour, and told that a bill would be introduced that afternoon that would be of interest to the Federation. The Federation saw the MCA as punitive. In its view, the Act was intended to give the government a new weapon to use in its struggle with the labour movement. This assessment may have been a complete distortion of the government's real intentions; but what the labour movement believed at that time is a historical fact even if it was false.

On the other side of the equation, the Social Credit government of the day distrusted the motives of the leaders of the trade union movement. The New Democratic Party was the political opposition, and the powerful British Columbia Federation of Labour openly allied itself with this party. Consequently the government never knew for certain whether Federation officers were speaking as labour leaders or as NDP politicians when debating the course that the labour movement would take in response to a government initiative.

This political uncertainty between labour and government manifested itself in a major confrontation when the MCA was introduced into the legislative chambers. Union leaders labelled the law 'punitive,' marched on the legislature, and threatened to boycott the Mediation Commission in protest. They condemned the new commission as a 'Gestapo dictatorship,' and denounced the Bill as 'Nazi, Fascist policies.'[9] The deep and bitter hostility generated against the Bill, even before it had passed third reading, gives credence to the opinion that, because of such resistance, the Mediation Commission was doomed to failure from the beginning.

These consequences of the introduction of the MCA point out a useful lesson about the process of reform of industrial relations. Where significant *group* rights are in issue in a democratic society it is imperative to develop a strategy of participatory legislative reform. Even well-founded attempts to regulate ·the balance of economic power in collective bargaining law may be rendered ineffective and unsuccessful by a unilateral process of reform, rather than by any lack of merit in the reform itself.

Non-political forces also influenced the direction of the MCA. The plan outlined in the Act can be attributed, in part, to a key study made in 1967, by Mr Justice Nathan Nemetz (as he then was), who had been appointed by the BC government to examine the industrial relations system of Sweden, a country which, at that time, was looked upon as a utopia because it had enjoyed more than forty years of un-interrupted labour peace.[10]

The Nemetz Report recommended establishment of a permanent industrial inquiry commission similar to the Mediation Commission – but with one very important difference: the tribunal should not have any compulsory powers to decide collective bargaining disputes through binding arbitration.

It would have been difficult to find the antecedents of compulsion in Sweden, where the right to strike over contract formation or inter-est disputes is universal, extending even to police, fire, utility, hospital workers, and civil servants. In any event, Justice Nemetz concluded that Sweden's remarkable success in settling labour disputes was *not* because of any special laws or procedures, but rather because of exist-ing cultural and social values and because of political factors.

At about the time the Nemetz report was published, the idea of using compulsion to solve public interest disputes was being actively pursued by some management leaders in British Columbia. The Hon. J.V. Clyne, chief executive officer of the largest lumber company in the Province, urged, in the midst of the 1967 forest industry strike, the creation of an independent 'fact-finding board' with the power to render binding decisions in the private and public sectors. Clyne ex-plained that 'The time must come eventually when labour disputes will be regarded as any other dispute between citizens, and will be carried before courts specializing in labour cases.'[11]

As an alternative to the right to strike, the proposal that labour courts give binding decisions has been favourably received in many quarters. A few months before Clyne recommended a labour court for British Columbia, Judge Samuel I. Rosenman of New York pro-posed a 'new judicial system of courts – labour courts' for the United States.[12] Judge Rosenman reasoned that the public respect and con-fidence enjoyed by the US judiciary could be transferred to such a system of labour courts, and he concluded that compulsory arbitra-tion would thereby become acceptable to the trade union movement.

The Rosenman idea received wide support. By October, 1967, bills were introduced in both the Senate and Congress to establish the 'United States Court of Labor-Management Relations.'[13] The Act would have created, in Washington DC, a labour court that would re-solve emergency labour-management disputes at the instigation of the president. The intent behind the Senate bill was that the labour court would be used only as a last resort.

Professor Archibald Cox of Harvard Law School testified against the idea before the Senate Judiciary Committee hearing the bill. Cox pointed to the failures of permanent administrative machinery established during the Second World War to end labour disputes without strikes. He predicted that a labour court would prolong labour disputes, rather than solve them, because 'No employer or union supposing itself to be within the court's jurisdiction would agree to any settlement upon the terms less favorable than the court imposed; it would simply refuse to agree with the opposing party and take the case to the court for an award.'[14] Having the judiciary render binding decisions 'where no one can honestly pretend that objective legal principles govern the decisions is bound to weaken the whole notion of law,' argued Cox. This point is particularly telling if there is defiance of the law, as experienced by the War Labor Board and compulsory arbitration decisions in Australia.[15]

Similar fears were expressed in the testimony of Derek Bok and John T. Dunlop, of Harvard University, who concluded that such a tribunal would inevitably be drawn into deciding national economic policy.[16] Although the criticisms of the Rosenman labour court were never proved, because the bill died after the Senate judiciary hearing, it is interesting to bear these concerns in mind when analysing the problems encountered by the BC Mediation Commission.

The title, Mediation Commission, is confusing because, as the tribunal held in an earlier decision, 'The Mediation Commissioners do not perform a mediation function.'[17] It is true that, under the MCA, an important part of the plan was the administration of independent research and the provision of mediation services, but these were performed by the mediation officers, not by the Commission itself.

The role of the Commission was much more like that of the labour court proposed by Judge Rosenman for emergency disputes in the United States. The court-like nature of the new tribunal was reinforced when the Minister of Labour introduced the bill in the legislature, and referred to the 'judicial system' as analogous to the role that the new Commission would perform.[18]

Provisions in the MCA for the constitution and administration of the Commission support the thesis that the authors of the law favoured a labour court over an administrative agency. There was no legislative guarantee that the appointments to the Commission would be equally representative of labour and management. Nor did the Act require a tripartite status for the Commission, this being the usual composition of *ad hoc* arbitration tribunals of labour-management disputes. Nevertheless, the first three commissioners were actually tripartite by experience.

Independence, the hallmark of the judiciary, was firmly established by (1) a legislative tenure for a renewable term not exceeding ten years, and (2) the requirement that commissioners would be disqualified for owning any securities in companies or for taking any benefit from a trade union that might appear before them.[19] To enhance the independence of the Commission, and in the hope of attracting the best qualified personnel, the salaries offered were extraordinarily high – more than those paid to either the Premier of British Columbia or the Chief Justice of the Supreme Court of Canada in 1968.[20]

The MCA required that the procedures followed by the new Commission were to be exercised with court-like formality for the '*judicious* disposition of disputes.'[21] Pleadings were assumed, and even the burden of proof was to be assigned at the 'inquiry' before the 'hearing' took place.[22]

That the government intended the labour court to follow a strictly judicial procedure was demonstrated by its first appointment of a chairman for the Commission. He was a Supreme Court judge with little or no experience either as an arbitrator or as a mediator of labour disputes. What he brought to the job was the status of a judge, rather than the skills of an expert in the field. The choice was a mistake, as later events would prove; it was perhaps the single most serious mistake made during the MCA experiment.[23]

With jurisdiction over both the public and private sectors, the Commission's primary function was to dispense binding decisions in disputes judged by the cabinet to be contrary to the 'public interest.' As section 18, the key provision for the private-sector, essential-services disputes stated:

'18 (1) Where a dispute between any employer or group of employers and his or their employees or a trade union is not resolved, and, in the opinion of the Lieutenant-Governor in Council, it is necessary, in order to protect the public interest and welfare, that
(*a*) no employee shall strike, and no employer shall lock out his employees; or
(*b*) an existing strike or lockout shall immediately cease,
The Lieutenant-Governor in Council may
(i) refer the dispute to the Commission;

(ii) Order that the Decision of the Commission with respect to the dispute, whether such Decision is given on a reference pursuant to paragraph (i) or otherwise, is final and binding upon the parties except to the extent that the parties agree to vary the same.

(2) An Order given under the section expires on all parties to the dispute signing and executing a collective agreement.'

The framers of the legislation had assumed that free collective bargaining, including the right to strike, would prevail for the resolution of the vast majority of disputes. The power of the Mediation Commission was intended for only those extraordinary cases in which it was necessary for the government to intervene to protect the public from harm.

The definition of an emergency under the MCA was very sparse. The cabinet could use the might of law to end strikes by finding only that they are against 'the public interest and welfare.' The lack of a more precise definition of emergency strikes was a source of criticism. 'Like the sword of Damocles,' inveighed an opposition member, 'we find the ominous power of the Cabinet brooding overhead with the possibility of unlimited, unrestricted, and perhaps even unfounded cabinet action.'[24] The Minister of Labour defended the Act by explaining that emergency disputes 'have not been defined because it is not possible to define all such disputes.' To prove the point he related the example of a maintenance strike in a hospital that would not be contrary to the public interest for the first few days, but if it lasted longer, then intervention might be necessary.[25]

The open-ended definition of the MCA resulted in an uneven application of the law by the cabinet. For example, an injunction was issued under section 18 against 55 electricians working in a single pulp mill in Port Alberni after only a six-hour strike, while no order was made when 28,000 workers in the forest industry were on strike for three weeks (see Table 1, p. 119). Although most of the orders under section 18 were in labour disputes causing only economic harm (and in some cases even economic harm was minimal) rather than injury to health or person, nevertheless there was broad public support for government interference in each instance.

In the public sector, section 19 of the Act provided that the government could refer any labour relations dispute in the civil service to the Commission for a hearing. The government was free to decide, either before or after the hearing, whether or not it would be bound by the decision of the Commission. This unusual discretion may be explained by the fact that, in 1968, civil service employees had only limited bargaining rights and strikes were illegal.

Municipal and hospital employees were treated by the Act as part of the private sector; and significantly, restrictions on the right of policemen, firemen, and hospital workers to strike were removed for the first time. The government had anticipated that these essential-service employees would not exercise their right to strike, but have their differences settled by the Mediation Commission.

The central idea of the MCA was attractive in its simplicity. Why should the public not have the benefit of a highly qualified, specialized tribunal, with the mandate to 'secure industrial peace and to promote conditions favourable to settlement of disputes.' (section 39) and to decide fairly on the basis of evidence (as a judge would do in ordinary civil cases) the controversy between two parties who cannot agree on the terms of a collective agreement? Almost like a fire-fighting service, the Mediation Commission was to be a permanent institution with the responsibility of preventing strikes contrary to the public interest. Why not a guardian of the public interest for essential-industry strikes?

No matter how sound an idea may be in theory, its success in practice is the critical measure of its true value. Indeed, in the 'jungle' of labour relations, success has been described as the only relevant principle. Measured against such a standard, the MCA was not a success.

From the beginning, there was a lack of confidence in the ability of the three-man Commission to perform its important task. Within a short time of the first appointments, the management representative and the director of research resigned under a cloak of secrecy but leaving the impression that the relatively unknown chairman did not have their confidence.

The first decision rendered by the Commission, after a hearing into a dispute concerning psychiatric nurses in the public sector, was followed by disenchantment. This first decision was significant because, although compulsory arbitration was anathema to the private sector, by contrast – at least at the beginning – the idea of arbitration by the Mediation Commission was welcomed by those public service employees who did not have the right to strike. The alternative for them was unilateral decision by the government; therefore, unlike the BC Federation of Labour, public employees initially were concerned that the Commission would not be used in their disputes – an attitude that changed immediately after the first decision.

Relations between the nurses and the government hospitals employing them had degenerated in 1967 to the point of threatened mass resignations. In the summer of 1968, shortly after the MCA was proclaimed, the cabinet ordered that selected issues in the nurses' dispute be referred to the Commission for a non-binding decision.[26]

After a hearing of evidence in September and October, the Commission handed down a ruling in November, holding in favour of the government on the issue of salaries and granting no pay increase to the employees.[27] As one might predict, the nurses were 'bitterly disappointed' with the decision.[28]

The situation worsened when the government, on issues other than salary, refused to implement the decisions that favoured the nurses. For example, the Commission had recommended a differential in pay for shift work that was not implemented in 1968, and that was still a grievance with the nurses in 1972. The incident was an unfortunate beginning, for it raised grave doubts about the Commission's impartiality and credibility.

After the decision on the psychiatric nurses, the government never again referred a public-employee dispute to the Commission. This was not considered any loss by the union leaders, who no longer sought the intervention of the tribunal. As the leader of the Government Employees' Association said later: 'We would now boycott the Commission if the Government referred a dispute to it.'[29]

One of the key benefits foreseen by advocates of the labour-court idea was the confidence that would arise through creation of a permanent arbiter of disputes.[30] Judge Rosenman thought the reluctance to use arbitration in collective bargaining disputes stemmed from the *ad hoc* manner in which three men are 'haphazardly appointed for one specific case,' and therefore, 'they have to begin from scratch and learn the necessary background.'[31] He assumed that, through the accumulation of experience and expertise, a permanent labour court would ultimately gain the esteem afforded courts of law. Unfortunately, instead of enhancing the Commission's prestige, permanency became one of the main causes of dissatisfaction.

The experience of the municipal police forces before the Commission illustrates the defect of institutionalized arbitration. Prior to introduction of the MCA, the police in British Columbia had a long history of solving their disputes by compulsory arbitration.[32] The arbitration boards for the police were created anew for each particular dispute. These *ad hoc* boards were usually of a tripartite composition, with each party's nominee selecting the chairman.

With the establishment of the Mediation Commission, the police were required to take their disputes to this body. Problems arose when the Commission decided against the police on certain issues of principle, such as the question of wage parity between the two major cities of Victoria and Vancouver. Because of its permanent composition, once the Commission decided against the union on the parity issue, it was predictable that, in order to be consistent, they would always decide against the union on this issue.

An editorial in the official publication of the union explained the discontent of the police: 'In effect the Mediation Commission Act has put the Police in the position of asking the same tribunal to reconsider their decision of the year before. This is a disheartening prospect for any organization seeking change ... the Mediation Commission Act seems to be alienating the one group in the community that supports compulsory arbitration. Any new legislation should return to the representative *ad hoc* board with the terms of reference presently in the Mediation Commission Act.'[33] Under the old system of *ad hoc* arbitration boards, there was always the opportunity to select a different nominee or chairman in the hope that he would reverse the decision of the previous year.

To protest against the MCA, a boycott of the Mediation Commission was ordered by the BC Federation of Labour, and many unions supported this tactic. As a result, there was no union representation at some of the hearings. Of this situation, the chairman remarked: 'The Commission has made it clear that it does not regard itself as having the power to compel the attendance of the parties, and it may proceed in the absence of a party if it chooses to do so. This applies even in a situation where the Government invokes section 18 of the Act, and orders the Commission to hold a Hearing and give a Decision which is binding on both parties. There is nothing in the Act empowering the Commission to require either party to attend, but both parties could be bound by the Decision regardless of whether they attended.' The effect of the chairman's approach to this problem was very damaging to the appearance of justice before the Commission.

In the absence of the union at the hearing, the procedure looked arbitrary, and resulted in decisions favouring management. The Commission tried to justify these decisions by saying: 'Because the 'burden of proof' of each of the matters lies on the Union, and the Union has presented no material whatever to us, there is no responsibility on the Employers to make any presentation on these matters. The Employers simply have no case to meet. If this appears on the face of it to work an injustice on the Union, we can only say that they are themselves the authors of their own misfortunes.'[34] Yet, when we recall that the union in the foregoing case was under a section 18 compulsory cabinet order to have its dispute resolved by a binding Commission decision, to fall back on a legalistic 'burden of proof' as an answer to the union's claims seems very unfair. Obviously, the waning credibility of the new institution suffered further damage.

Some unions chose to ignore the Federation's boycott of the Commission. The non-affiliated Teamsters union initially stood apart from it, and adopted a responsible attitude toward the idea of the MCA. As a Teamster official explained: 'Since we now have it, both parties had better decide what their approach is going to be. Are we going to drive the cabinet into making decisions whether this, that or the other industry is of such vital public interest that strikes will not be allowed? Are we going to force the government into the election of compulsory arbitration to settle disputes? Or are we going to try to devise some approach whereby the two parties will start building bridges toward one another with a view to doing all that can possibly be done to sort out their problems? I would make a serious appeal to both sides to start putting their own house in order, and not continue in the way that leads to intervention of third parties. If we can't bring ourselves to do this, then we don't have a right to be critical of those who must govern in the interests of all society.'[35]

Despite this support, one of the first compulsory cabinet orders in the private sector was issued *inter alia* against the Teamsters because of strikes in the construction industry. When the decision came down, the union was completely taken aback; in a very unusual move, the Commission had offered a wage increase that was *less* than the final offer made by the company. Subsequent to strident attacks on the decision in the media, the cabinet ordered the Commission to reconsider its decision, which it did – without varying the wages.

The Commission defended its breach of the unwritten rule that an arbitrator stays within the bounds of the parties' negotiations, on the grounds that the company's last offer was made after strike notice was given in the hope of preventing a work stoppage. Because a strike did occur, 'the parties were no longer bound by their offers and counter-offers when the dispute was heard by the Commission.'[36]

Perhaps there is a logic that supports the decision of the Commission in the Teamsters case, but it is a logic devoid of reality. When that case ended, the Teamsters, like the Federation of Labour, thereafter boycotted the hearings of the Commission.

As a result of the growing concern over the competence of the Commission, a pattern began to develop whereby parties faced with the threat of government intervention would opt instead for *ad hoc* arbitration. During a school strike in Vancouver in 1970, for example, the Minister of Labour publicly announced that he would not permit the strike to continue beyond the current week, or he would use cabinet powers to order a return to work under section 18, with a binding decision by the Commission.

The union resisted the threatened order and, just before the Commission was called upon to adjudicate, offered to return to work if the School Board would agree to submit the dispute to binding arbitration by an independent third party. The School Board agreed, and Dr Noel Hall, an experienced industrial relations professor from the University of British Columbia, was chosen for the task. By this eleventh-hour device, the union avoided appearing before the Commission.

The lack of confidence in the ability of the Commissioners to solve labour disputes ultimately became so widespread that, by 1971, even the government that had authored the MCA boycotted its own creation. Threatened by a public utility strike at BC Hydro, the government invoked section 18 of the Act, and ordered the employees back to work; but the order did not allow the Commission to intervene.[37] Instead, the Hon Mr Justice Nathan Nemetz was appointed as an *ad hoc* arbitrator of the dispute under the research section of the Act.[38]

A major problem with the interventionist approach of the MCA was the disrespect shown by employees for compulsory back-to-work orders issued by the cabinet. To ensure compliance, the law relied on court penalties as sanctions. Fines of up to $1,000 could be levied against individuals, and $10,000 for companies and unions, or $150 a day for continuing offences. Also, the injunction and contempt of court could be the penalties imposed for the disobeying of compulsory orders.

The experience of using the law to prevent strikes in BC proved that it does not follow that, because strikes are illegal, they will not occur. As Bok and Dunlop warned: 'Compulsory arbitration creates serious risks that workers will refuse to comply with unpopular awards and will rebel, either by stopping work or by various covert tactics, such as slowdowns, sabotage, or working to rule, which can cripple the efficient operation of modern industry.'[39]

The first enforcement problem arose out of the first use of binding arbitration in the private sector. The construction industry had been involved in a lockout-strike situation for three months, when the dispute was declared against the public interest, and the employees were ordered back to work. The proclamation was issued on Saturday, 18 July, 1970. But on Monday, only two unions, the Teamsters and labourers, reported for work. The other unions, including the bricklayers, carpenters, insulators, operating engineers, and plumbers, ignored the cabinet order and refused to return to work.[40]

The Federation of Labour threatened a general strike if anyone was fined for disobeying the law. No one was prosecuted. The employees resumed work a week later, after the personal intervention of the Premier, who helped convince the disputants to let an arbitrator of their own choice settle the dispute.[41] Notwithstanding these breaches of the law, no charges were laid against the employees or their union.

The second confrontation occurred two years later, once again in the construction industry. This time, when the employees defied the back-to-work order, the government responded by laying charges under the Act. The RCMP raided the offices of a number of the unions involved, seizing documents in a search for evidence of wilful disobedience of the law. On the basis of these searches, charges were laid against four unions. The search warrants were later quashed, however, and all seized documents were ordered returned to the unions on the grounds that the warrants were issued without reasonable cause to believe the unions were breaking the law.

Later, some of the charges were dismissed because of the Crown's failure to prosecute, and the remaining charges were stayed by the new NDP Attorney-General because of the repeal of the MCA. The Attorney-General warned, however, that the stay should not be interpreted as condoning violations of the law.[42] The employees did not go back to work until at least a month after the compulsory order was issued. In the face of stiff penalties, there was a widespread and open defiance of the law – a sobering reminder of the limited effectiveness of the judicial order of social problems.

The reluctance of the government to prosecute offenders of the law may have an unhealthy impact beyond the pale of industrial relations. It is the view of some that to permit wilful defiance of the law by labour will have a deleterious effect on the whole fabric of society.[43] The late Justice Ivan Rand concluded that the flouting of the law with impunity by workers, 'has a significance beyond labour relations; it involves the enforcement of laws generally. An established contempt for one field of regulation spreads its blight to others.'[44]

The experiment with a strike control tribunal on the model of the MCA in British Columbia must be viewed with great misgiving. The Mediation Commission failed miserably to generate confidence in compulsory arbitration of public interest disputes, and it alienated even those groups that had previously supported *ad hoc* compulsory arbitration.

The Mediation Commission acted like a labour court and as a result political confrontation with the trade union movement increased and the incidence of strikes increased also.[45] Because the Commission lacked credibility, important disputes were referred to *ad hoc* arbitration. The back-to-work orders by the cabinet were ill-timed[46] and treated with open defiance by employees. Eventually the failure of the MCA contributed to the defeat of the Social Credit government at the polls.

Following the demise of the MCA, shortly after the defeat of the Social Credit government in 1972, a new design for labour law was required for the province. For this purpose, the Minister of Labour established a task force of three special advisers from outside government to advise him on what reforms were needed.

The Special Advisers first set up an office, solicited briefs from all interested parties, and held meetings for several months. Hearings also took place throughout the province, and the advisers travelled across Canada to study the comparative experience of other jurisdictions. After completing this process of involving the interested parties and the public, the advisers reported to the minister, and he introduced a bill in the Legislature titled the Labour Code of BC.

On the issue of public interest strikes, the provisions of the new Labour Code are vastly different from that of the MCA. Under the Code, all employees – including police, firefighters, and hospital workers – have a right to strike. Initially, there was no strike control by law of public interest disputes. The basic approach of the new law was to reduce legalism in the response to labour-management controversies, follow a policy of non-compulsion, and to rely on mediative devices to protect the public interest.

After the Labour Code was first introduced, Dean Arthurs wrote an analysis of its provisions, and summed up the philosophy of the law as follows: 'It is evident the architects of the Code intended not so much to provide 'cures' as to urge, cajole, even coerce the parties, in their own interest and in the public interest, to exercise self-restraint and to practise mutual accommodation.'[47]

When the Labour Code was debated in the Legislature, the opposition was very critical of the failure to include any legal restraints on strikes by public sector unions representing the police, firefighters, and hospital workers. A special provision was made to allow these workers binding arbitration at the union's option, and it was hoped that they would take advantage of this alternative. This option did not deprive them of the right to strike. Critics have exclaimed that it would be unthinkable for the police to go on strike.

The answer of the Minister of Labour to these critics was that standing prohibitions have proved ineffective under the MCA, and therefore his approach to the problem was to look in another direction for solutions. The new direction indicated was for the law to provide curative rather than punitive measures to protect the public interest. 'What legislatures and courts can do to change the habits of people in industrial relations must in democratic societies always and everywhere be limited,' said Professor Otto Kahn-Freund. And this advice was taken to heart in the law reform of industrial relations in British Columbia in 1973.

Although it is true that curbing strikes by law may be possible within narrow limits, experience has demonstrated need to expand the horizon of public attention beyond using the sanctions of law as a remedy for the strike problem. The reality is that the labour relations problems of strikes, picketing, and slowdowns are not legal phenomena. They are symptoms of social problems. Changing our perspective from legal rights to social obligations means that we can see the distinction between these two questions: should policemen have the right, in law, to strike? should policemen strike?

More importantly, if the standing law of labour relations is facilitative rather than coercive, it should dissuade the public from viewing labour-management conflicts in strictly legal terms and from relying on a legal solution of these problems. When problems are viewed from a social perspective, it is natural to place emphasis on administrative rather than legal solutions. An administrative approach to industrial relations should place concern on the underlying problems of employees who perform jobs in the public interest.

I call your attention to three examples of the implementation of this approach in British Columbia: 1. We have established a reformed Police Commission that is independent of government and staffed with people who are highly qualified to reorganize the service in a more enlightened way;[48] 2. A special commission has just been set up under the direction of Dr Hugh Keenlyside to hear the problems of firefighters and recommend solutions; 3. In the hospital field, an industrial inquiry commission has made recommendations – to all interested parties – to alter the structure of collective bargaining in an effort to improve the fairness of the process. The foregoing efforts are not generally viewed as remedies for strikes that are against the public interest, but I believe that they will be helpful for this purpose, and should be counted as part of the strategy of industrial peace.

Another increasingly important preventive device that the literature of industrial relations has left largely unexplored is the office of the Minister of Labour. Relying on the prestige of his position, and the experience of his senior staff, the Minister may play a significant role in the resolution of public interest disputes. Ministerial intervention can be useful in a variety of ways.

First, the Minister may introduce mediation into a dispute that has not had the benefit of this service. Mediation is a voluntary service in British Columbia. If neither party seeks this kind of assistance, then the right to strike is not barred. But, in the public interest, a mediation officer may be appointed by the Minister. Sometimes this is necessary because neither party wishes to appear to show weakness in asking for mediation.

When a mediation officer has been appointed, a statutory strike bar comes into effect until he reports to the Minister.[49] The law allows the Minister to extend the appointment of the mediation officer, and thereby extend the strike bar. In practice, this power should be used with restraint. Our method is to extend the appointment only if both parties agree that it would be helpful. What is often forgotten is that our mediation service has achieved a very high record of settlements.

Another successful *ad hoc* device for heading off public interest disputes has been the use of an industrial inquiry commission. This is an extraordinary remedy, and it is only available at the discretion of the Minister. The relevant section of the *Code* states:

'1. The minister may, either upon application or on his own motion, make or cause to be made such inquiries as he considers advisable respecting industrial matters, and, subject to this Act and the regulations, may do such things as he considers necessary to maintain or secure industrial peace and to promote conditions favourable to settlement of disputes.

2. For any of the purposes of subsection (1), or where in any industry a dispute between employers and employees exists or is likely to arise, the minister may refer the matters involved to a commission, to be designated as an "Industrial Inquiry Commission," for investigation and report.

3. The minister shall furnish the Industrial Inquiry Commission with a statement of the matters concerning which the inquiry is to be made, and, where an inquiry involves particular persons or parties, shall advise those persons or parties of the appointment.

4. Following its appointment, an Industrial Inquiry Commission shall inquire into the matters referred to it by the minister and endeavour to carry out its terms of reference; and, if a settlement is not effected in the meantime, it shall report the result of its inquiries, including its recommendations, to the minister within fourteen days after its appointment, or within such extensions of time as the minister may grant.

5. Upon receipt of a report of an Industrial Inquiry Commission relating to any dispute between employers and employees, the Minister shall furnish a copy of each to the parties affected, and shall publish it in any manner as he considers advisable.

6. An Industrial Inquiry Commission shall consist of one or more members appointed by the minister.

7. An Industrial Inquiry Commission shall, during its period of appointment, have the power and authority of a Commissioner under sections 7, 10, and 11 of the Public Inquiries Act.

8. Where, either before or after an Industrial Inquiry Commission makes its report, the parties agree in writing to accept the report in respect of the matters referred to the Industrial Inquiry Commission, the parties are bound by the report in respect of those matters.'

Prior to 1972, in British Columbia, the legislative machinery for this kind of intervention existed, but it was never used. During the past two years, however, the industrial inquiry commission has been employed on twenty-two different occasions, and the results have been very encouraging.

Despite the history of the MCA, and the doctrinaire attack on compulsory arbitration by the unions, a surprising development has been the substantial number of times that labour and management have both agreed to be bound by the decisions of an industrial inquiry commission. In five major disputes during the past two years, both parties agreed *in advance* to be bound by whatever decision was given by an industrial inquiry commission.[50] Voluntary binding arbitration was the result.

Collective bargaining is a dynamic process, and third-party intervention must be flexible if it is to be effective. For this reason a new technique called 'med-arb' has been used by industrial inquiry commissioners in BC. This process basically involves the commission's mediating the dispute and encouraging the parties to arrive at their own settlement, under pressure of knowing that if they do not, then the Commission will change hats and render an arbitration award.

Clive McKee, who was chairman of six major inquiries, explained: 'In the past year, as an Industrial Inquiry Commissioner, I have experimented with this technique and have found that my experience ranged all the way from a position where I was left no alternative but to write a binding award to a position of just keeping the pendulum in motion while the parties settled, in great detail, their own agreement. As a negotiator, mediator, arbitrator this is the system of dispute resolution that I advocate. Voluntary Med/Arb.'[51] The 'med-arb' technique is an informal administrative process, sharply different from the legalistic procedures followed by the Mediation Commission.

The *ad hoc* approach of the last two years has gained the confidence of labour and management where permanent machinery did not. One reason is that the chairmen could be selected on the basis of their particular experience in the area of the dispute. During the two-year period, seven different chairmen, with leading reputations in industrial relations, were appointed to resolve the various disputes. The *ad hoc* choice of commissioner did not allow stultifying precedents to be made. The air of uncertainty that resulted gave everyone the feeling that they had a chance. This experience underscores the criticism directed against a permanent mechanism or tribunal – like the Mediation Commission – as a guardian of the public interest.

Reliance on the Minister of Labour to settle disputes personally can be very destructive of the collective bargaining process if it is not handled carefully. Stanley Hartt, a Montreal lawyer, has attacked the federal government's misuse of ministerial intervention, pointing in particular to the highly publicized, personal intervention of Bryce Mackasey when he was Minister of Labour in 1968. Hartt explained that high level mediation was counter-productive because, 'people have learned that by being tougher they scare the politicians into remedial action.'[52] The parties hold back making concessions until the last possible moment which may be when the labour minister personally intervenes. Hartt warned, 'The more interventions they get the more the minister has to intervene and the less he accomplishes.'

While the above criticism may be true, it does not detract from the need for intervention when vital public services are on strike. Timing and judgment will reduce the counterproductive effect of ministerial intervention, as explained by Stanley Hartt. However, as with many choices in life, there is no perfect answer and compared with the damage of a dispute, ministerial intervention is usually the lesser evil.

Essential to the Minister's discretion concerning intervention under the Labour Code is the principle of voluntarism. The Minister has no authority to make the award of the industrial inquiry commission binding on the parties unless they both agree. Indeed, as a rule of practice, the Minister has refused even to appoint such a commission unless both parties agree. This leaves the timing of the intervention in the hands of the participants – and those familiar with collective bargaining know how important timing is to the resolution of labour disputes.

It is true that the voluntary approach of the Labour Code will not resolve all disputes against the public interest. Considerable success in achieving industrial peace, however, has been due to the finality of the existing law, with no step or remedy beyond mediation or an industrial inquiry commission (which must be consensual). The hard reality of compromise must be faced early.

There is ultimately one other step to be taken in any major dispute: the Minister of Labour can introduce *ad hoc* special legislation to deal with a specific crisis affecting the public interest.

Commenting on the Labour Code's approach to protection of the public interest, Dean Harry Arthurs cited the difficulties connected with reliance on special legislation: '*ad hoc* legislation is a dangerous business: it invites politicization of disputes; it changes the rules in the middle of the game – and is thus liable to be challenged on grounds of basic fairness; and it does not afford the parties or the government any long-term basis for resolution of difficult, structural problems. Moreover, for a government which generally looks to labour for support, reliance upon *ad hoc* legislation may simply not be a realistic possibility. This point was seized upon by an opposition spokesman who pointed out that during a ferry strike prior to the introduction of the Code, the government had conceded that it had a gun at its head, that it could do nothing. The new Code leaves the government's position unchanged.'

The picture may not be as bleak as Dean Arthurs paints it. First, of course, it can be argued that although *ad hoc* legislation may be imperfect, like old age, the alternative is worse – witness the MCA experience with standing legislation. Second, the NDP government has not shown the reticence to legislate that Arthurs predicted. During 1972, three special laws were introduced to deal with labour disputes affecting the public interest.[53]

The most serious threat to the Labour Code's policy of non-compulsion occurred when firemen in four Vancouver suburban municipalities went on strike in August 1974. Unlike their counterparts in Victoria, the Vancouver unions failed to take advantage of the special option of binding arbitration. After mediation failed, they did agree with their employer to the intervention of an industrial inquiry commission. An experienced commissioner, Jack Sherlock, was appointed, but the unions rejected his non-binding recommendations.

Subsequent to a last-minute effort by the Minister to mediate the dispute through his office, these firemen went on strike. In a surprise move, they refused to offer life-supporting services, such as ambulances and inhalators. In one municipality, even the telephone service was left unanswered so that fires could not be reported. Because of the immediate danger to life and property posed by this disastrous turn of events, the Legislature was called into special session, and the Essential Services Continuation Act was introduced. The effect of the Act was to end the firemen's strike by compulsion.

As part of this special Act, the Labour Code was also amended to allow, by cabinet order, a 21-day cooling-off period when strikes in essential services endanger health and safety.[54] The Minister explained in the House that the intent of this amendment was to provide time for the parties to reconsider their position before the government was required to draft *ad hoc* legislation ending their dispute.

Many critics concluded after the firemen's strike that the Labour Code's policy of non-compulsion was a failure. 'NDP's strike policy goes up in smoke,' headlined the newspapers, and editorials urged law reform: 'Hopefully, British Columbians have seen the last act of a sordid little drama that earned no applause from any quarter ... . The government's duty is clear. It should amend existing legislation to make a recurrence of such an emergency impossible. Otherwise it is as derelict as the firemen.'[55] So we have come full circle. Only two years earlier, the media had written off legislation as the answer to emergency strikes. 'Make it work or get rid of it' summed up public dissatisfaction with MCA in the last year the law was in force.

The firemen's strike showed that voluntarism is not the final answer,[56] but it is important to remember that the special back-to-work legislation was obeyed. By contrast, compulsory orders under the MCA were openly flouted. Timing is everything in collective bargaining, and the timing of strike prohibitions may be a significant ingredient in their effectiveness. The lesson may be that in this difficult area the law will have the most force and effect when it is tailored to the particular dispute.

CONCLUSION

I began this discussion by asking the question: what role should the law play in meeting the problem of strikes in essential service? I was concerned about the experience in British Columbia with standing legislation administered by a tribunal of the judicial model. The negative experience under the MCA should make one pause and reflect upon the efficacy of using legal remedies with standing prohibitions against strikes.

It should be realized, however, that the MCA experiment in British Columbia was not conducted under laboratory conditions. The law was abruptly introduced without any participation of labour who considered it punitive. The labour movement's unwavering antipathy toward the tribunal, together with the boycott of its hearings, greatly weakened the credibility of the Commission's decisions.

Looking back over the four-year history of the MCA, the Commission appears to have pursued a course of self-destruction in the decisions it made. It displayed an insensitivity toward the dynamics of labour relations from the first case of the nurses, where no salary increase was given, to the Teamster case, where management won more than it sought.

The law was defective in not defining criteria for an emergency dispute, and the cabinet made some injudicious decisions as to what strikes were against the public interest, and issued compulsory orders on insufficient information.

In light of these human errors, it could be asked whether the basic concept of the law was ever tested. If a different chairman had been selected and other changes made to the Act, would the law have succeeded? I doubt it. Compulsion through law is a fragile process, depending greatly upon the timing of the intervention for its success. With standing emergency legislation like the MCA it was too easy to find that a public interest strike should be declared illegal. As a result the force of law in labour relations was weakened.

In fact, the irony is that permanent machinery will be less effective than an absence of legislative machinery, because the certainty of a fixed solution becomes part of the problem in collective bargaining as it discourages genuine negotiations until the final and known solution is invoked by the government. After carefully considering the dilemma, W. Willard Wirtz observed: 'One possible conclusion from the debate about whether 'emergency labour disputes' should be handled by injunction, seizure, compulsory arbitration, fact finding, or mediation is that the answer to this riddle lies perhaps less in any one of these devices than it does in all of them. Increasing emphasis is being placed upon "flexibility" as the essential quality in any satisfactory governmental approach to national crisis resulting from a collective bargaining stalemate. The key feature of a number of recent proposals is that the executive agency charged with responsibility in this area should be authorized to invoke, in a particular case, not a single preordained procedure but rather any one of several procedures.'[57] The experience of the past eight years in British Columbia has shown the need for more thought and greater sophistication about the kind of issues and decisions, related to formal legal processes, and the kinds that ought to be left to social and administrative processes.

While the reform of the Labour Code chose voluntarism over compulsion, however, the introduction of special legislation in the firemen's dispute shows that the policy of non-compulsion is limited only to *standing* legislative machinery. The Code relies on the difficulty of introducing *ad hoc* legislation and the uncertainty of its content as an impetus to the settlement of labour disputes. The law recognizes the restraint that must be exercised by the government if its intervention is going to be successful in the resolution of labour disputes. Only experience can judge the success of the Labour Code and while the initial signs are certainly more favourable than at this same time under the MCA, it is still too early to predict the outcome.

Realistically, there is no satisfactory answer to the dilemma of public interest disputes and the role of government. There are serious disadvantages to either option discussed in this paper. While I do not agree with the depth of Ed Finn's pessimism in his recent articles in the *Labour Gazette*[58] about the future of the institution of collective bargaining, I do believe that he was very accurate in describing collective bargaining as an 'adversary concept' where an 'underlying assumption has been that the best way to resolve differences between unions and employers is through trial by combat, and that the attendant disruptions are a small price to pay for bargaining freedom.'

The assumption of this paper has been that the options are to find different ways of protecting the public interest within the existing economic system of collective bargaining. Perhaps collective bargaining is the real devil and our efforts should be directed towards alternatives to the collective bargaining system, recognizing the destructive force of the adversary approach in industrial relations.

DISCUSSION

Crispo Thank you, Jim. Your paper seems to break down into two or three areas. To begin, we should spend a few moments on alternatives to collective bargaining and strikes. As you suggested we could also examine the role of *ad hoc* and permanent law as well as the role of the Minister of Labour and inquiry commissions. Then we could turn to the broader question of how open and public the negotiating process should be, particularly in the public and essential industry sectors.

Waisglass A very fundamental question has been raised: what will replace collective bargaining? I find Alan Flander's definition of collective bargaining quite realistic. He defines it, as I recall, as a bilateral system of private self-government, involving essentially a political process of rule-making and rule-enforcing in the governing of employee-employer relations. I agree with him also that the only alternatives are either unilateral rule-setting and rule-enforcing, by either the employer or the union, or the determination and enforcement of the rules governing employer-employee relations by the state. Now if you agree with that, then I think you will agree also that voluntary arbitration is an extension of the collective bargaining system because it is controlled by the parties themselves. But compulsory arbitration is an antithesis of collective bargaining because it is essentially state determination.

I have found Mr Matkin's paper very interesting and attractive, showing a great deal of conceptual strength and practical wisdom in the evaluation of the experience of the BC jurisdiction.

I agree with Mr Matkin that the right to strike is an inevitable and necessary part of the collective bargaining system. The right to strike and lockout is essential if workers and employers are to have the rights to both attempt changes and to resist changes in the criteria by which wages and other rules are to be determined. If both parties are to retain the rights to both initiate and resist changes in the rules, or in the criteria by which the rules are being set, then strife situations are inevitable consequences of the process of adjustment to change. If either or both parties are restricted in their rights to initiate and resist change, we would have even deeper and more serious conflicts, but without the effective and constructive mechanisms of adjustment that are provided by the free collective bargaining system.

The restriction of collective bargaining by restricting the right to strike means state determination of wages and other terms and conditions of employment. And if the state expands its decision-making functions in the labour market, it will inevitably have to assume similar responsibilities in other markets. Of course, strikes can be eliminated; but are we prepared to pay the price? And the most important part of the price cannot be determined financially: what price do we put on freedom?

Bairstow I can't resist commenting on one system which I observed personally for a year. Compulsory arbitration, as practised in Australia, is touted to be an alternative to strike. Under that system the power relationships don't change. They're basically not different from the union-management power relationships in North America. Strong unions simply use the system as a minimum or a base. Collective bargaining is then utilized to add other benefits on the base. The government regulations based on awards simply form a floor to the settlement. Such a system may perpetuate the weak unions since they can get along merely by accepting the awards. The weak unions and the government may find it more comfortable to work together.

The other point I want to make is that in a situation where labour laws are unpopular and unions are strong, their restrictions are ignored. The problems aren't solved with high financial penalties or jail sentences for violations. Although compulsory arbitration appears on the surface to be an alternative to strikes, in reality it is not.

The point that I want to emphasize – and this probably stems from my North American bias – is that the Australian system provides inadequate opportunities for leadership on both sides of the table. Because of the overdependence on government advice and intervention a very small number of people may really be calling the shots. Those of us who are concerned about shopfloor training and the development of second-string leadership deplore the absence of opportunities for leadership development.

Carter On the question of collective bargaining being the only approach, I think one should distinguish between the collective bargaining process and employee participation. I think that employee participation in the process of wage determination is, and should be, here to stay. But I'm not sure that in the public sector, employee participation in wage determination follows the collective bargaining model that we have in the private sector. I think we should be aware that there is a substantial difference since the game being played in the public sector is a more political game. What you have is a type of employee lobbying.

In many cases wage determination does not depend on economic considerations. Take the case of the nurses and nursing assistants where the main employer is the government. We have this notion that somehow nurses should be paid more than nursing assistants. What is the notion based on: market forces or value judgment? I think, to a very large extent, it is based on value judgments, and these value judgments create an employee pecking order. Of course, value judgments are often adjusted; I think that's one of the problems that we face right now during a period of inflation.

Given my assumption that the game is a political one, the question is whether the techniques of private sector bargaining are appropriate. As I look at private sector bargaining, at least in Ontario, I see the primary technique being conventional mediation. The dispute is regarded as a private dispute between the parties. Government intervention is restricted to mediation, with the mediator simply trying to bring the private parties together. I wonder if this approach is appropriate in the public sector where you obviously have appeals being made to the public, especially by the bargaining agents. I would suggest that greater use be made of fact-finding – that someone should be sent in to investigate the dispute, and make the facts known to the public. This may pave the way for later governmental intervention, which in many cases is going to be necessary, but the public might as well know the facts in advance.

A second technique that might be used is a compulsory employee vote, so that before the employees can go on strike, they have to vote on the last offer of the employer. If they vote in favour of the employer's offer then it becomes the collective agreement; if they vote against it, then they can go on strike. This may be important because I think bargaining agents are often ahead of the members of the bargaining unit and may be raising the expectations of employees to an unrealistic level.

Thompson I think that all of the experience of the last few years indicates that bargaining agents are *not* ahead of their members. Furthermore, the last-offer-vote is a sucker play for labour leaders.

Johnston I agree with you that the last-offer-vote can be abused and so perhaps it should be structured a bit. However, we had an interesting experience with the last-offer-vote in the Ontario Hydro dispute three years ago. Management was convinced that the leaders were ahead of the members and therefore were reluctant to move. Finally after a lot of pushing and shoving over three months, there was a membership vote and the members voted to stay out on strike. Even though the vote was only 55 per cent in favour of remaining on strike, that's all it took to make management review their position. So there will be occasions when such a vote is of more use in influencing the employer than the union and its members.

Aaron Let me first respond briefly to the last point. I would say that as far as the United States is concerned, your observations are totally refuted by the years of experience since 1948, when the first emergency dispute under the Taft-Hartley Act occurred. Our experience with votes on the employer's last offer shows that employees have never voted to accept the employer's last offer. Usually the offer is rejected by overwhelming percentages, almost invariably upwards of 90 per cent, except in those instances in which the workers have completely boycotted the vote, as was the case with longshoremen and maritime workers. The last offer simply does not work for any number of reasons, one of which is that it is impossible to get on one ballot some of the very complex issues that are involved. I have served as chairman of boards of inquiry under the Taft-Hartley Act, and I can assure you that there's no way that you can put an entire pension plan or a whole seniority system on a ballot in such a way that anyone could intelligently vote.

The notion, at least in the United States, that union leaders are ahead of the workers is a fond delusion of Congress that has been exploded over and over again. The truth is that the leaders generally tend to be more conservative than the rank and file.

I'd like to get back to what is perhaps the most fundamental issue raised in this seminar, namely whether there are workable alternatives to collective bargaining. We've had really two kinds of suggestions. We've had the suggestion that there just may be some better procedures, and I agree that the number of those options is quite limited. We've also had the suggestion that perhaps we should look to see if we can't eliminate the causes of disputes, thereby eliminating the necessity of establishing a procedure to deal with them. I don't believe that this is possible. I believe in the inevitability of enduring conflict between managers and those who are managed in any system anywhere in the world, including the people's paradise in eastern Europe.

So we're really left with either unilateral determination by the stronger party or government intervention. The latter option, in certain systems such as those of continental Europe, has been very effective. I am referring to the establishment, by constitution or by statute, of all the basic conditions of employment, while leaving scope for a certain amount of collective bargaining above the non-waivable minimums. I suppose that if we had a government ruled by platonic guardians who were all-wise and all-knowing, they could simply set all the terms and conditions of employment at an optimal level; but that doesn't seem to me to be possible. So I come to the conclusion, paraphrasing Winston Churchill's comments on democracy, that collective bargaining has so many weaknesses and so many different deficiencies that one is hard put to say anything in its favour except that it's probably better than any other system that has been devised to deal with these problems.

I agree with Buz Woods that it is possible to have collective bargaining within a policy that outlaws the right to strike. I also share his reservations about the efficiency or equity of such a system, but it certainly is possible. Moreover, I do not think that strikes always involve an argument over the appropriate dispute resolution criteria. There are some strikes that arise simply because the parties can't agree on the facts of the situation. I recall in that connection the statement of William H. Davis, the chairman of the National War Labor Board in the United States during the Second World War, that parties could not really be in disagreement over facts – they could only be in ignorance of them. That is, of course, where fact-finding might be helpful.

At the other extreme there are attempts to use collective bargaining to accomplish things which it cannot accomplish, such as the complete redistribution of income. Those who would use collective bargaining, or more particularly the strike, for that or similar purposes are really engaging in political action quite different from ordinary bargaining.

My final point is that one explanation for the variety of feelings of dissatisfaction or disappointment with collective bargaining is that we have different expectations of what collective bargaining can or should do. I remember Dexter Keezer, an American economist who sat as a public member on the National War Labor Board and who described collective bargaining as an excessively-praised system of bluffing, bulldozing, and groping toward an inaccurate decision that ought to have been reached with hairline precision. Well, of course, if that's the standard for evaluating collective bargaining, it obviously fails. But my feeling about Dexter is that his were the problems of a good man in an imperfect world; you can't expect perfection from collective bargaining any more than you can expect collective bargaining to cure any number of ills, from unemployment to racial discrimination. But I think that the system is as good as we're likely to find if we don't expect too much from it.

Steinberg Lindblom, in 1947, suggested that unions and capitalism were incompatible. Nevertheless, if one summarized the labour experience for Canada since the Second World War as ably as Professor Aaron has done for the US, I think we would all concur in accepting an aging, imperfect collective bargaining system, when faced with the alternative to age. Some disenchanted trade unionists in the late 50s and early 60s didn't agree. Paul Jacobs, Paul Sultan, and to a lesser extent Sol Barkin produced titles like 'Old at 28'; perhaps the further implication was 'Obsolete at 30.' From the perspective of another fifteen years, we are now suggesting that while it is always worthwhile theoretically to look at the alternative, there may not be one.

Professor Aaron intrigues us with the possibility of some platonic gentlemen capable of setting wages with such exquisite accuracy that all our democratic feelings are simultaneously satisfied. But short of this platonic ideal, if we tamper with the market forces as translated through the collective bargaining process, we are doing something far more profound than is realized. Just for a moment note that the Canadian labour force stands at just under 10 million. It is dispersed among some 15,000 or more occupations spread across four thousand miles of the country. This is accomplished without state intervention, or a computerized system having determined precisely where, and by whom these jobs should be filled, or under what circumstances, and more important at what pay rates.

Surely there are frictions and immobilities in the labour market process. John Porter shows us that the Canadian ethnic mosaic is vertical and ranked so that social and economic mobility is certainly limited. The over 6 per cent unemployment rate is another grim reminder of labour market imperfections. Yet the mechanism that has ultimately caused this vast and generally rational distribution of human resources to take place is in fact wage-setting in its market context. If we seriously tamper with that process we'd best think of a central planning alternative for the whole allocation process. In this, I think Harry Waisglass' suggestion about freedom of choice and freedom of alternatives becomes critical.

It is interesting to note that notwithstanding all the alleged pressure and wage distortions from collective bargaining, over the course of fifty years or more, labour's share of national income has not changed very much. The 10 per cent increase in Canada in over the last two and a half decades can be attributed mainly to changes in the occupational distribution. Perhaps only 2 per cent of that increase in labour's share can be attributed directly to the effects of trade unionism. Of course, this does not mean that trade unions have not ushered in great changes, and have not performed important functions.

I would suggest that in contemplating an alternative to collective bargaining in the public sector and essential services generally, we are considering a very comprehensive, drastic alternative such as central planning of the allocation of all human resources, since a piecemeal or makeshift alternative might distort the entire economic and social structure. Some may feel that a reordering of the entire society is desirable. Nevertheless, the really incompatible partnership is that of unions as we know them and of central planning, not of unions and capitalism.

Phillips I find this whole discussion about alternatives a bit unreal. The whole collective bargaining system, going back to the nineteenth century when collective bargaining was born, is based on a civil contract between the parties as to the distribution of an economic surplus. It can only exist in an economy dominated by civil contract relationships. As I think Harry Waisglass mentioned, the only alternatives are either unilateral determination or third party determination. In the latter case it is no longer a civil contract but becomes a contract determined by the state or by a public authority. The parties become recipients rather than contributors to the contract-determining process.

One alternative that has not been discussed is workers' control such as exists in Yugoslavia and in modified form in Sweden. In certain cases, management has accepted a measure of workers' control, apparently with successful results from the points of view of both shareholders and workers. Wages, productivity, and profits have all increased and demarcation and management rights disputes have decreased. This supports the thesis that when a number of disputable issues are removed from the bargaining process, then conflict is less likely simply because there are fewer items to cause disagreement.

Recent university experience provides as illustration. Until recently, universities have had a form of workers' control. As long as fees were determined by the university there was considerable harmony. Now the university has little control over fees or other finances. As a result, the real employer is the provincial government. This decrease in workers' control has led to a corresponding increase in conflict. I think this is also happening with the growth of the civil service, particularly at the senior levels where administrative controls have become more bureaucratic.

Adams I want to talk about dispute-resolving procedures, and I want to address a question to Jim Matkin because he said he was in favour of an *ad hoc* approach to disputes in contrast to standing legislation. What worries me about *ad hoc* solutions is that if we assume the parties to be reasonable and want an accommodation, how can we assist in the communication? I think Jim's comment about the timing is accurate. Timing is important, but by depending on *ad hoc* solutions to particular disputes, isn't the dispute going to have to rear its head before it is identified and action taken? However, if bargaining relationships were monitored at an earlier point in time, wouldn't some of those problems be identified early? In other words, when it comes time to appoint an inquiry commissioner, there's a real risk that it will be too late. The parties may have already made public statements and thus placed themselves in a corner. When communications break down it is often a serious dispute and I would think many wish they had the chance to solve the problem at an earlier point in time. If the problem were spotted earlier the authorities could provide a neutral, experienced, trusted person to facilitate communication and to work with the parties over time. In other words, could not each relationship have its own industrial relations doctor when needed, whether it comes through the Minister's office or whether it's a result of a standing tribunal. Is there any role for what I'm suggesting in the *ad hoc* approach? I'm worried if the answer is no.

Matkin I don't see any cause for concern because what you propose is not contrary to the *ad hoc* approach. They are not mutually exclusive; they are mutually compatible.

Woods I'd like to come forward with some specific proposals without running into too much detail. First, we should recognize that the private model doesn't work in some areas of the public sector. It doesn't work because in some situations a failure to continue with the service doesn't hurt anybody except the employees on strike and perhaps ultimately the government. On the other end of the spectrum the private model doesn't apply because the consequences of a breakdown are more than the public can tolerate.

We have recognized that pre-legislative formulae will not work in a great many cases and may indeed aggravate the situation. We should also recognize the importance of the element of consent for the procedures that are going to be used. One of my criticisms of government is that they have played God and written rules and regulations about how collective bargaining should work in the public sector without sufficient consultation with the involved parties and the public.

There should be some way of encouraging a new set of institutions which would place emphasis on two things: first, that the parties jointly accept responsibility for the public consequences of their actions, and second, that the parties be free as far as possible to design their own procedures to reduce the possibility of public hurt. I'm referring here to instruments of joint consultation and bargaining over procedures rather than bargaining for conventional agreements. I agree that *ad hoc* legislative solutions must be retained. However, I also feel that this approach to the solution of particular bargaining disputes is no longer enough, and that attempts to legislate procedures to protect the public have not been satisfactory. This leads me to the simple conclusion that the parties themselves should be given the freedom to design things that will work, and that they may need some prodding or pressure.

Carrothers I bring the latest word from Plato's Republic. I was assigned the task of explaining why the Task Force recommended the creation of a Public Interest Disputes Commission. Theoretically, there is a minimum of four reasons, given that the Task Force consisted of four members; and knowing its members, there could be five or six reasons.

Remember that we were sitting in 1968 – a time when *ad hoc* legislation had been used in a number of cases that left people very alarmed. We had been appointed in 1967 basically because of the *ad hoc* legislation that was introduced to settle the railway strike in 1966. The year 1966 was one of the worst for work stoppages in a very long time. In fact work stoppages in 1966 were approximately one-half what they were in 1974! It was also a period of extreme tension and bewilderment because of the conflict of roles of the government. The government was vulnerable because it had to face the dilemma of government as employer and government as sovereign. Words like public interest, public policy, and politics, were very much in the air and we know that the meaning of those words are rooted in the shifting sands of values.

Feeling strongly pressed to devise an alternative to *ad hoc*ery in public service disputes we decided to go into a collective trance. We put Abbé Dion in the chair for the time being and then engaged in hyperventilation for a few minutes and eventually made contact with MacKenzie King's mother. She said she would 'ask my boy Willy,' who was after all the authority on these things, and we eventually obtained a penetrating glimpse into the present. It was necessarily transient. We decided to try to find some means of bringing aid to the political process, without usurping the function or responsibility of politicians in the circumstances where the government as sovereign must supersede the government as employer. The Public Interest Disputes Commission was the product of our collective judgments. It was rejected by labour, management, and government, largely because they didn't think that the country contained the requisite platonic guardians to compose the commission. It was, in other words, viewed as unrealistic. This indicates that we must take the political process and the behaviour of politicians as a given and recognize that there is a good deal of theatrics in the political process, including the posturing, grandstanding, and upstaging, to say nothing of the use of cosmetics. Particularly, in the wage-price issue there is probably a need for an external stimulus to the political process within parliament.

My own thinking is that *ad hoc* legislation is not as bad as people perceived it to be in 1966, and within our political process it may be a perfectly legitimate choice to make in the determination of procedures for the containment of a public interest dispute.

Crispo Are you still in favour of a Public Interest Disputes Commission?

Carrothers Not if it is not acceptable to the primary parties.

Crispo As chairman, I'll refrain from making the strong defence that can still be made for such a Commission.

Waisglass The Matkin paper and some of Buz Woods' comments underscore a fundamental principle in industrial relations: the possibilities for reducing the incidence of strikes are greatly enhanced where the parties themselves have formulated the procedural rules. Apparently, in BC the parties themselves were meaningfully involved in developing the present legislative framework which now gives them the broadest scope for determining their own procedures for dispute settlement. As I have said, this approach is based on a well-established but not-too-widely-known principle. Perhaps, in order to strengthen our knowledge and understanding, we should not only examine the causes of strikes, but undertake again the enquiries of a few decades ago into the causes of industrial peace. We should be examining the experiences with voluntary arbitration, the most recent examples such as in the US steel industry, and the oldest examples, in the needle trades.

I doubt if anyone here would dispute the claim that there is a great deal more stability in industrial relations systems where the parties determine their own procedures and are alert and active in keeping them in a good state of repair by changing them, experimenting, and looking always for improvements. I think this is one of the basic principles that Harry Arthurs had in mind in his study for the Woods Task Force, and what the Woods Task Force had in mind when it recommended the establishment of a Public Interest Disputes Commission. I know that the failure to implement this recommendation has caused some disappointment among the academics, but I think that it should be acknowledged that some of the functions that were foreseen for such a commission have been carried out reasonably well by officials in the federal labour department. Consider the major innovation which they encouraged and assisted the railway companies and unions to introduce last year: a unified negotiating procedure embracing all bargaining units for all of the railways. I believe that the most useful and effective accomplishments of the federal mediation and conciliation staff are that they have been able to persuade the parties in many situations to examine their procedural rules in between contracts and to improve and strengthen them before the next negotiating rounds.

Arthurs It seems to me that what is clearly needed is some pluralistic view of the solution to the problems. It's foolish in the extreme to think that a single prescription can solve all disputes for all industries, at all periods of time, for all personalities, and in all political situations. What is needed is pluralism.

I thought that my suggestions to the Task Force were useful in terms of encouraging the parties to devise their own solutions. I think that's terribly important. By 'parties' I mean not just labour and management generically but labour and management in particular industries at particular moments in time. I believe we ought to direct their attention not simply to resolution of a dispute which has already begun, but to bargaining about the development of agendas and ways of working out their relationship with or without the assistance of third parties.

I think the issue is confused when we suggest *ad hoc* legislation to be the only way to achieve a pluralization of solutions. Indeed I am about to make the argument that there is very good reason for not depending on *ad hoc* legislation.

In the first place, stimulating the parties well in advance of the dispute to address the issue of developing their own particular solution has, if nothing else, a Hawthorn effect, a highly desirable effect which will generate goodwill and ingenuity.

Secondly, the possibility of a particular *ad hoc* response to a dispute being well conceived and of permanent use, is minimized when it is conceived and imposed after the parties have already been hammering at each other for a very long time. Furthermore, building any basis for a better relationship is lost by *ad hoc*ery.

Thirdly, the obvious and proper criterion that any government and any Minister of Labour would use in developing *ad hoc* legislative solutions is the political criteria – that which is conceived to be in the best interest of the state, or the best interest of his party's view of the best interest of the state. That is appropriately the criterion to which he will respond, but it is not the criterion to which the parties have been responding up to this point in time or to which they will be required to respond in the future. Their criterion is what is in the best interest of the particular industrial relationship. Those two criteria – the government's and the disputants' – may or may not coincide; in fact there is a very substantial risk they will diverge. I think that the risk, therefore, of applying totally different criteria is very substantial.

Moreover, there is considerable bias in our system generically against changing rules in the middle of the game. Obviously there are times when it has to be done but it's not something which one can advocate as a common practice.

Finally, if nothing else, I make the crass argument of expediency. I question the notion that the Minister of Labour is the right person to determine policy, and the cabinet to bring legislation forward to parliament.

NOTES

1 For one of the best Canadian references see Arthurs, *Labour Disputes in Essential Industries*, Canadian Task Force on Labour Relations Study no. 8, 1970 (with a comprehensive bibliography at 255-64); see also, J.A. Finkelman, *Employer-Employee Relations in the Public Service of Canada* (1974); Phillip Cutler, 'Permanent Labour Courts in the Light of the Rand Report and the Woods Report, *Can. Bar Ass. Papers* 332-49 (1969); *Ontario Royal Commission Inquiry into Labour Disputes* (1968) The Honourable Ivan Rand Commissioner; *Report of Swedish Labour Laws and Practice* (to the Hon. L.R. Peterson QC, Minister of Labour, BC & Mr Justice Nathan Nemetz, Commissioner (1968 Commission)), Woods, 'Canadian Policy Experiments with Public Interest Disputes,' 14 *Lab. L. J.* 739 (1963); Anton, *The Role of Government in the Settlement of Industrial Disputes in Canada* (1962); Woods, 'Cana-

dian Collective Bargaining and Dispute Settlement Policy: An appraisal,' 21 CJEPS 447 (1955); Carrothers, *Collective Bargaining Law in Canada* (1961)).

2 D.E. Cullen, *National Emergency Strikes* 2 (1968).

3 Arthurs, *supra* Note 1, at 10, quoting Chamberlain and Schillings, *The Impact of Strikes: Their Social and Economic Costs* 252-3 (1954).

4 SBC 1968 c.26.

5 SBC 1972 (2nd Session) c.8.

6 SBC 1973 c.122.

7 Labour Law: *Old Traditions and New Developments* 79 (1967).

8 RSBC c.384. As Paul Phillips reviews the history of its introduction in his *No Power Greater*, 'In 1959 the Bennett government introduced Bill 43, a new Trades-Union Act, to replace the 1902 statute. The Bill outlawed sympathy strikes, secondary boycotts, and picketing, except during a legal strike, and the publication of "Do not patronize" lists even during legal strikes. Special provision was made for both notice and Ex Parte injunctions. The legislation limited a wide area of civil liberties relating to free speech, even where the information being communicated was factual. The act was condemned by a number of lawyers and even by a member of the judiciary. However, the legislation was upheld in the courts, and it became evident to labour that it could only be repealed by political action.'

9 Statement of Stanley Little, President of Canadian Union of Public Employees, reported in the *Vancouver Sun*, 24 Feb., 1968. A Canadian politician charged: 'Since Lincoln emancipated the slaves, no man has been forced to work against his will.'

10 *Report of Swedish Labour Laws and Practice* (1968) and, T.L. Johnston, *Collective Bargaining in Sweden: A Study of the Labor Market and its Institutions* 154-5 (1962).

11 Mr Clyne made the proposal in a meeting of the Men's Canadian Club of Vancouver reported in the *Financial Post*, 16 Dec., 1967.

12 'A Better Way to Handle Strikes, Newsday, 15 July, 1967. His idea is explained in *Proposals to Deal with National Emergency Strikes*, Legislative Analysis no. 3, American Enterprise Institute for Public Policy Research (1969).

13 Hearings before the Subcommittee on Improvements in Judicial Machinery of the Committee on the Judiciary, US Senate, 90th Congress, 1st session, on s.176 providing for the establishment of a United States court of labor-management relations, 17 Oct., 1967, Washington DC, 1968 (cited as Hearings). This Labor Court should be distinguished from proposals for a Labor Court of Appeals such as Professor Morris suggests in his article, 'Procedural Reform in Labor Law – A Preliminary Paper, 35 *J. Air L. & Com.* 537, 544-50 (1969). The Morris Labor Court would be created to supplant the NLRB

and not to decide emergency disputes. See also Florian Bartosic, Labor Law Reform – The NLRB and a Labor Court, 4 *Geo. L. Rev.* 647 (1970).

14 Hearings, at 94-5.

15 D.W. Oxnam, 'Industrial Arbitration in Australia: Its Effects on Wages and Unions, 9 *Ind. Lab. Rel. Rev.* 611-13 (1956); J.E. Isaac, *Compulsory Arbitration in Australia*, Task Force on Labour Relations Study no. 4 Ottawa (1968); J.N. Timbs, *Towards Wage Justice by Judicial Regulation: An Appreciation of Australia's Experience under Compulsory Arbitration* 107-121 (1963); G.H. Sorrell, 'Industrial Relations in New Zealand' 3 *J. of Ind. Rel.* no. 2 (Aust. 1961) reprinted in Northrup, *Compulsory Arbitration and Government Intervention in Labor Disputes* 331-46 (1966).

16 *Labor and the American Community* 239 (1970).

17 *Bd. of Police Comm. of Victoria* v *Victoria City Policemen's Union* (Reconsidered) 23 Aug. (1969).

18 The Hon. Leslie R. Peterson, Excerpts from Remarks on the Second Reading of Bill 33 (1968), 11.

19 a. *id.* s.14. See Watts, 'The Adequacy of BC Labour Legislation,' 5 UBC *Law Rev.* 251, at 200; and *supra* note 27, s.29.

20 In 1968 the Premier's salary was $20,000. Constitution Act SBC 1965 c.6 s.2(1) plus $16,500 *id.* s.3(1). Supreme Court judge was $26,000. Judges Act RSC c.s.1 s.13.

21 S.40.

22 S.13(a) and (c).

23 The chairman's impartiality was questioned as a result of a public speech in which he urged that 'under no circumstances' should civil servants have the right to strike and on another occasion he raised labour's ire by promising a vigilance against 'sneak strikes.' These speeches prompted a newspaper editorial to describe him as 'the Spiro Agnew of BC Labor-management relations,' *Vancouver Sun*, 9 Jan., 1969, 4. Only a few months after the Commission was established another editorial concluded: 'What astonishes most people has been the way the commission itself behaved since its creation. Confidence in its capability – already shaken by labour's attack – has been further undermined by the way the commission has bumbled and blundered from one unhappy headline to another, to the considerable embarrassment of the government.' *Vancouver Sun*, Dec. 1968.

24 Garde Gardom (Liberal, Vancouver Point Grey Member of Legislature).

25 Peterson, Excerpts from Remarks, Second Reading of Bill No. 33 (1968), 13.

26 Order-in-Council 2360.

27 *Psychiatric Nurses Assoc.* v *Civil Service Commission*, 14 Nov. 1968.

28 *Vancouver Sun*, 16 Nov. 1968.

29 John Fryer, Statement made during interview with writer 14 Aug. 1972.
30 *Supra* n.13.
31 *Ibid.*
32 *Municipal Act,* TSBC 1960, c.255, s.194; R.A. Herbert. 'Some Comments on Bill 33,' 26 *The Advocate* 188 at 198 (1968).
33 T.E. Wolfe, 'Quo Vadis,' *Thin Blue Line,* 3, 1, 1 Jan. 1971 (Official Publication of the BC Federation of Peace Officers).
34 *Aero Transfer Co. Ltd.* v *General Truck Drivers & Helpers Union,* Local 31, 26 March 1971, 3.
35 *Ontario Royal Commission Inquiry into Labour Disputes* 69 (1968).
36 *Lafarge Concrete Ltd. et al.* v *Bldg. Mat. Const. & Fuel Truck Drivers Union,* 18 July 1970 (reconsidered 11 May 1971); *Lafarge* case, *supra* n. 142. The company's last offer was 88 cents increase for a 7½ hours day. The Commission awarded 75 cents for an 8 hour day. *Vancouver Sun,* 7 Nov. 1969.
37 An editorial in the daily newspaper referred to the 'shattered dignity' of the Commission and concluded: 'The provincial government has now openly by-passed its own commission, at least partially because the IBEW, backed by the BC Federation of Labor, refused to appear before it. Aside from the political aspects of this boycott, the union directly concerned had some color of merit for its decision. Both its employer, BC Hydro, and the Commission are creatures of the government. The union could argue that the commission's impartiality would be clouded by the inter-connection.' *Vancouver Sun,* 2 July 1971.
38 '(1) The Commission may from time to time, with the approval of the Lieutenant-Governor in Council, appoint or engage experts and persons having special or technical knowledge necessary for the purpose of assisting the Commission to carry out the provisions of this Act. (2) Every person so appointed shall disclose to the Commission any interest, direct or indirect, which he may have in any matter coming before the Commission.' C26, s.34.
39 *Labor and the American Community* 240 (1970).
40 Order in Council 2444. The confrontation received front page coverage. The headlines in the newspaper read, 'Some Unions Defy Back-To-Work Order,' *Vancouver Sun,* 20 July 1970. The plumber's union threatened to down tools across the province if any of them were fined for disobeying government order. Their agent said, 'We know we are breaking the law but we won't go back without a contract.' *Ibid.,* 21 July 1970. On defiance of the law an editorial concluded: 'As this week dawns British Columbians are asking themselves whether the apparatus of their democracy has become unmanageable. Is the rule of law to be set aside by decree of the BC Federation of Labor? The BC Fed. as it is known familiarly among its office-holders and bosses, says yes.'

41 The parties agreed to return to work and let the Deputy Minister of Labour, Bill Sands, mediate the dispute. His efforts were not entirely successful and a month later there was a further breach of the no-strike order. *Vancouver Sun*, 19 Aug. 1970.

42 *Vancouver Sun*, 21 and 23 Sept. 1972. The Attorney-General said: 'I'm concerned that nobody would take the staying of these charges as an indication that the laws of the province should not be upheld. Of course they must be.'

43 Bok and Dunlop ask, 'is it wise to impose fresh and uncomfortable controls [such as compulsory arbitration] in a period when respect for law is already so precarious in so many different areas of life.' *Supra* n.2, at 240-41.

44 *Ontario Royal Commission Inquiry into Labour Disputes*, at 66-7.

45 In 1970, there were 1,683,261 man-days lost because of labour disputes, which is five times as many days as 1967.

46 See Table 1, which shows data about the compulsory orders made by the cabinet under s.18.

47 'The Dullest Bill: Reflections on the Labour Code of British Columbia,' 9 UBC *Law Rev.* 280, at 340 (1975).

48 SBC 1973.

49 S.60.

50 These disputes were in the mining industry, hospital industry and railroad, chemical plant, and oil industry.

51 Address by Clive McKee, 10 Dec. 1974, 'Arbitration of "Rights" and "Interests" Disputes.'

52 *The Province*, 10 Dec. 1974, 'Ottawa Action Hindering Strike Settlements.'

53 First law arose out of a municipal dispute creating a flood danger, Kamloops Emergency Flood Control Act; the second was the Essential Services Continuation Act ordering back to work Vancouver Municipal Firemen; the third imposed an Industrial Inquiry Commission award on the Elevator Constructors Unions.

54 SBC (1974), c.122: '(7) Where a dispute between an employer and a firefighters' union, policemen's union, or hospital union is not resolved, and as a consequence an immediate and serious danger to life or health is likely to occur or is continuing to occur, the ·minister may recommend that the Lieutenant-Governor in Council, by order, prescribe a cooling off period of time not exceeding 21 days during which period no employee or trade-union shall strike and no employer shall lock out his employees or during which period any existing strike, or lock-out shall be suspended. (8) The Lieutenant-Governor in Council shall not make an order under this section more than once in respect of the same dispute.'

55 *Daily Colonist*, 10 Aug. 1974.

56 Ed Finn explains the problem as follows, 'You and your governments have thus backed yourselves into a corner. And the dilemma in which you now find yourselves was perfectly illustrated by the recent experience of the Government of British Columbia, which, after extending the right to strike to municipal firemen, had to rescind that right when some firemen tried to exercise it. The point is that, whether firemen and other essential workers have the legal right to strike or not, governments can't ignore the threat to public health and safety that the withdrawal of their services eventually creates. But the converse is also true: if such workers feel sufficiently aggrieved, they will strike as a last resort, regardless of the legality or illegality of their Action.' *Labour Gazette*, 74, Nov. 1974, 769.

57 'The Choice of Procedures Approach to National Emergency Disputes,' in *Emergency Disputes and National Policy*, Irving Berstein, Harold L. Enarson, and R.W. Fleming, eds., 149 (1955).

58 'The Adversary System is Dead – But it Won't Lie Down,' Ed Finn, *Labour Gazette* 74, Oct. 1974, 694; 'Proposal for Labour-Management Peace in the Public Sector,' *Labour Gazette* 74, Nov. 1974, 767.

TABLE 1
Data on use of compulsory orders under s.18 of the MCA

Industry	Parties to dispute	Date and no. of compulsory order	No. of employees	Extent of industry involved	Length of strike or lockout	Area of impact	Nature of damage from stoppage	Decision by Commission
Police	Oak Bay Police Commission and Police Association	15 Sept. 1969 OC #2925	325	Limited	No stoppage	One city	Threatened	No
Cement	Lafarge Concrete et al. (3 employers) and Bldg., Mat., Const. & Fuel Truck Drivers Union	18 July 1970 OC #2443	500	Substantial	Three months	Province-wide	Economic	Yes
Construction	Const. Lab. Rel. Assoc. & Const. Trades Union	18 July 1970 OC #2444	25,000	Substantial part	Three months	Province-wide	Economic	No
Pulp and paper mfg.	Alberni Pulp & Paper Ltd. & IBEW Local 230	25 Sept. 1970 OC #3211	55	One pulp mill	Six hours	One city (10,000 pop.)	Economic	Yes
Transportation	Auto. Trans. Lab. Rel. Assoc. & Gen. Truck Drivers & Helpers Union 31	26 Feb. 1971 OC #661	3,500	56 general cartage companies (approx. 80% of industry)	One week	Province-wide	Economic	Yes
Public utility	BC Hydro & IBEW Local 258	30 June 1971 OC #2346	2,000	Electrical workers only	Nine days	Province-wide	Threatened	No
Hospital service	BC Hospitals Assoc. & RN Assoc. & Hosp. Employees Union 180	19 Jan. 1972 OC #210	16,000	Substantial part	No stoppage	Province-wide	Threatened	Yes
Building	Const. Lab. Rel. Assoc. & Const. Trade Union	14 June 1972 OC #2165	6,000	Approx. 20% of industry	Six weeks	Province-wide	Economic	Yes

BENJAMIN AARON

Procedures for settling public
interest disputes in
the essential and public sectors:
a comparative view

This paper is concerned, generally, with disputes over interests, as
distinguished from disputes over rights. Whereas the latter typically
involve disagreements over the meaning or application of a legal rule,
whether established by collective agreement or by statute, the former,
sometimes rather misleadingly referred to as 'economic disputes,' may
be said to arise out of unreconciled differences over aims and objectives, over hoped for improvements or restrictions in present terms
and conditions of employment.

This distinction is important because, in the majority of countries
in which it is observed, different methods of settlement have traditionally been prescribed for the settlement of the two types of disputes. Thus, in North America the preferred, if not exclusive, method
for settling disputes over rights is by arbitration; whereas interests
disputes are frequently, if not always, settled by conciliation and
mediation, or by industrial action in the form of strike or lockout and
related economic pressures.

The most conspicuous exception to the general observance of the
rights-interests dichotomy is to be found in Britain, where that distinction has never been taken seriously or observed in practice. Every
dispute, regardless of its theoretical classification, is treated simply as
a problem to be solved by the most effective means at hand. A claim
raised during the life of a collective agreement which is not covered
by its terms will not be rejected for that reason, as it normally would
be in the United States. Instead, it may be settled by adding a new

provision to the agreement, after the union has resorted to some form of industrial action normally associated with interests disputes.

The British practice is largely explained by three traditions. The first is that collective agreements are unenforceable in the courts. Even under the short-lived Industrial Relations Act, 1971, which created a 'conclusive presumption' that every collective agreement made in writing after the effective date of the Act was intended by the parties to be a legally enforceable contract unless the agreement contained a provision to the contrary, most employers and unions chose to include such a provision in their agreements. This rejection of legal sanctions as a means of insuring compliance with agreements is inconsistent with a sharp distinction between legal rights and economic interests. The second tradition is that collective agreements are 'open-ended,' i.e., they have no fixed duration. Under this arrangement, it is inevitable that disputes will arise over whether, for example, an action taken by one party or the other is covered by the existing agreement or constitutes the introduction of a new term or condition. The British do not invest this problem with any special significance; but in the railroad industry in the United States, in which there is a similar tradition of open-ended agreements, and in which a distinction is recognized between 'major' (interests) and 'minor' (rights) disputes, the obvious difficulty of determining when a dispute is major or minor has led to much litigation. The issue assumes an added importance, not present in Britain, because minor disputes in the railroad industry are subject to compulsory arbitration, whereas major disputes may eventually lead to a strike.

The third tradition, a natural offspring of the first two, is the refusal by British trade unions voluntarily to give up the right to strike in return for a commitment of employers not to lock out and for an agreement that all disputes over rights shall be submitted to arbitration.

Failure to observe the distinction between rights and interests disputes in terms of the procedures used for their settlement does not, however, invalidate the observation that both types of disputes exist in all societies. This is true even in the socialist countries of Eastern Europe, despite their official position that no conflict of interest exists, or ever can exist, between the directors of undertakings, representing the state, and the trade union committees, representing all the workers in each enterprise. Soviet doctrine, for example, maintains that all the persons concerned are representatives of the working class as a whole and exercise in its behalf functions, which although quite distinct, have only one purpose: to increase output and to raise the material and cultural level of the workers. But as Professor Otto Kahn-Freund has observed: 'Any approach to the relations between management and labour is fruitless unless the divergency of their interests is plainly recognized and articulated. I am persuaded that this is true of any type of society one can think of, and certainly of a communist as much as a capitalist society. There must always be someone who seeks to increase the rate of consumption and some who seek to increase the rate of investment. The distribution of the social product between consumption and investment can only be determined by a constant and unending dialogue of powers, no matter whether this takes place at the bargaining table, in Parliament, or in the recesses ... of government offices.'

The principal focus of this conference is on a limited variety of interests disputes, namely, those in the 'essential and public sectors'; accordingly, the discussion in this paper will be confined to methods of resolving those particular types of disputes. For comparative purposes, occasional references will be made to law and practice in Britain, France, Germany, Italy, and Sweden.

THE QUESTIONS OF ESSENTIALITY AND EMERGENCY

The concept of essentiality has its origin in attempts to mitigate the effects of strikes and lockouts in the private sector. The reasons are readily apparent. First, in most countries the right to engage in industrial action in interests disputes was won much earlier in the private sector than in the public sector, where it is still much more restricted. Second, in many European countries, the special status of certain types of public officials resulted in their being denied the right to strike. Finally, it was formerly assumed in most countries that all government services were uniformly essential and thus could not be permitted to be interrupted.

In the private sector, however, distinctions are sometimes made between run-of-the-mill and so-called emergency disputes. An emergency, by definition, involves essential goods or services. In general terms, an emergency dispute is one in which the disputants can hold out longer than the public. That circumstance provides the rationale for some kind of interference by the governmental authority for the purpose of preventing the strike or lockout or ameliorating its effects.

The approach to this problem in the United States is well known.

Two federal statutes contain specific provisions relating to emergency disputes. The Railway Labor Act (RLA), applicable to interstate railroad carriers and airlines, treats as an emergency any dispute which threatens 'substantially to interrupt interstate commerce to a degree such as to deprive any section of the country of essential transportation service.' If the National Mediation Board (NMB), the federal agency administering this part of the statute, concludes that such a dispute exists, it notifies the President of the United States, who then creates an *ad hoc* board 'to investigate and report respecting such issue.' The board thus created is supposed to 'investigate promptly the facts as to the dispute and make a report thereon to the President within thirty days from the date of its creation.' After the creation of the Board and for thirty days after it has made its report to the President, no change, except by agreement, may be made by the parties to the controversy in the conditions out of which the dispute arose. Strikes and lockouts during this period are, of course, prohibited; but after it has elapsed, unless Congress intervenes, both parties are free to resort to industrial action.

The Labor Management Relations (Taft-Hartley) Act, 1947 (LMRA) applies to all industries affecting commerce except those covered by the RLA. The emergency disputes procedures may be invoked by the President whenever in his opinion a threatened or actual strike or lockout 'affecting an entire industry or a substantial part thereof' would 'imperil the national health or safety.' If he so concludes, he may appoint an *ad hoc* board of inquiry, which is charged with the duty to report the facts and the issues in dispute. The board is expressly forbidden, however, to make recommendations. Upon receiving the board's report, the President may, and usually does, direct the Attorney General to petition a federal court for an injunction against the strike or lockout, and the court may grant the injunction if its findings accord with the President's opinion, which they almost invariably do. After the injunction has been issued, the board of inquiry is reconvened; and if the dispute remains unsettled, the board must submit another report without recommendations at the end of sixty days setting forth the efforts made to settle the dispute, the current positions of the parties, and the employer's last offer. Within twenty days following submission of the board's second report, the National Labor Relations Board (NLRB) polls the employees by secret ballot on their willingness to accept the employer's last offer and certifies the result to the Attorney General. Whatever the outcome of the vote, the Attorney General must ask the court to discharge the injunction, and the court must grant that request. Thereafter, unless Congress intervenes, both parties are free to resort to industrial action.

Experience under these two laws reveals some of the problems inherent in the concept of emergency or essentiality. The declaration that an emergency exists may be supported by acts justifying such a conclusion, but if so, the support is largely irrelevant. The declaration of emergency is, essentially, a political decision, and is as much a reflection of the incumbent President's temperament and style as of the actual or potential economic impact of the dispute. By way of illustration, we may note that the restrictive words 'affecting an entire industry or a substantial part thereof' have not prevented the President from invoking the LMRA procedures in a dispute involving only one plant of one company. Similarly, the statutory standard, 'imperil-[ing] the national health or safety,' has proved to be very elastic. It did not, for example, prevent the Supreme Court, in another emergency dispute, from maintaining an injunction based on a finding which, in effect, equated 'national health or safety' with 'the material well-being or public welfare of the Nation.'

On the whole, one is justified in concluding that, so far as the United States is concerned, it has been impossible to achieve consensus as to when a dispute truly imperils the national health or safety. If purely economic criteria are applied, few cases meet the test; but the line between emergency and inconvenience is frequently hard to draw, and public resentment against strikes in key industries, regardless of their effect on the national health or safety, is a political force that often cannot be ignored.

Presidents of the United States, in times of perceived emergency, have sometimes resorted to various *ad hoc* forms of intervention. These include appointment of special fact-finding boards (as distinguished from Taft-Hartley boards of inquiry or RLA emergency boards) with power to mediate and to make public recommendations; use of troops to do the work of strikers; and seizure of plants. There also appears to be no constitutional impediment to legislation conscripting strikers, although in 1946 the Congress refused to enact such legislation when requested to do so by President Truman.

Seizures of private plants were made in both world wars pursuant to the President's wartime powers as commander-in-chief of the armed services, or under the authority of special legislation. In 1952, however, when President Truman ordered seizure of a number of steel plants, after the steel companies had rejected a settlement proposed by the National Wage Stabilization Board to resolve a dispute with the steelworkers union, a majority of the United States Supreme Court held the taking to be unconstitutional in the absence of an express legislative mandate.

In Sweden the determination that a labour dispute is 'dangerous to society' is, typically, made by the bargaining parties, rather than by the government. Nor are there any statutory standards to guide the parties. In the basic agreement of 1938, between the Swedish Employers' Confederation (SAF) and the Swedish Confederation of Trade Unions (LO) the parties agreed that the Labour Market Board (consisting of three representatives of each party) should promptly consider any dispute referred to it by either party for 'protection of the public interest' or by 'a public authority or other similar body representing the public interest' in order 'so far as possible to prevent labour disputes from disturbing essential public services.' The parties further agreed to implement immediately any decision reached by a majority in a public-interest dispute.

In the Federal Republic of Germany, the Bonn Basic Law, as amended in 1968, defines various situations in which the government may intervene directly. Among these is included an 'imminent danger to the continued existence of the liberal democratic basic order' of either the federal government or of one of the constituent states. To allay the fears of the trade unions that these provisions of the Basic Law, as interpreted by the Federal Constitutional Court, might permit executive or legislative action against major strikes, the Basic Law was amended to provide that measures must not be directed against labour disputes which are carried on by associations in order to maintain or improve labour and economic conditions.

The critical word here is 'association' (*Vereinigung*), the question being whether that term covers unofficial groups as well as unions. Although that question is much debated by German lawyers, the prevailing view is that *Vereinigung* includes only a permanent official trade union, especially inasmuch as the Federal Labour Court has already declared 'unofficial' strikes to be unlawful. Moreover, according to orthodox opinion, a strike is not legal unless it can be settled by a collective bargaining agreement. Disputes which give rise to an 'imminent danger to the continued existence of the liberal democratic basic order' are not likely to meet that test.

In any event, there is a tradition in the German labour movement, dating back to the Weimar Republic, of unilateral, voluntary control in emergency situations. Briefly, the labour movement has recognized the need to protect the public interest against grave excesses of strike action in enterprises 'vital for life.' This policy was one of enlightened self-interest; for the German unions desired to avoid the use of para-military groups for 'technical emergency service,' which they correctly perceived as an instrument for breaking strikes.

The policy was reaffirmed at the end of the Second World War. In 1949 the rules of the Federation of Trade Unions were amended to provide special procedures in the case of industrial action affecting 'plants vital to sustain life, such as food or production, gas or water supplies, sewage, public health, funeral, traffic or coal mining enterprises, etc.' Before industrial action is taken, main union boards must report to the Federal Board the reasons for such action, its nature and planned extent, and plans for execution of emergency work in case of strike. If the Federal Board believes that the public interest involved requires it to do so, it will take any measures necessary to settle the dispute by conciliation. No industrial action may commence or continue until such measures have been exhausted.

Under this policy, all German unions have rules requiring their members to perform emergency work prescribed by the Federal Board. A refusal by a member to execute such work is considered a 'grave violation of duty' punishable by expulsion. Although there are no cases on the subject, the prevailing opinion is that a union which failed to maintain emergency services would be liable in a tort action for damages or, possibly, subject to an injunction.

In Italy and France, where the trade union movements are fragmented, the situation is quite different. Most of the Italian statutory law relating to essential services applies to employees engaged in 'service of a public character.' There is, however, a body of law applicable to a particular social situation, regardless of the private or public status of the workers involved. For example, the government has a general power to use military forces for public purposes. This power, which does not embrace either conscription of strikers or requisition of property, permits continuation of work halted by strikes, such as operation of public transport. Troops have occasionally been used even to milk cows.

In addition, local authorities (e.g., the mayor or prefect of a district) have considerable powers in respect of matters connected with public health, housing, and local police affairs. Also, if a service is declared by an administrative order to be essential for public purposes under the Penal Code, then it becomes a crime punishable by imprisonment for three or more public officials or private employees performing public services or employed in public service enterprises or those essential to public needs to leave their work collectively or to act in any other way which disturbs the continuity of work. Included in the covered group of private employees are attorneys and medical personnel.

In France a large area of emergency law has fallen into disuse. In the period between the two world wars the government possessed the power to conscript and mobilize strikers. This power was replaced by the authority of requisition. Although usually applied to public servants, this authority extends to all employment. Disobedience of an order of requisition amounts to more than serious misconduct (*faute lourde*); it is also a crime. However, the government may make such an order only in respect of 'persons employed in a service or an enterprise regarded as indispensable to provide for the needs of the nation' (*les besoins de pays*). This power is not considered by the courts as a limitation on the right to strike; but the administrative courts and, ultimately, the *Conseil d'Etat* (the supreme judicial body in the hierarchy of administrative courts) will confine the exercise of power to the limits of *les besoins de pays*.

The procedure consists, first, of a decree made by the Council of Ministers. Next, the minister concerned issues an order (*arrêté*); and finally, on the basis of that order, the prefect at the local level serves the orders of requisition on the workers.

In addition to the power of requisition, the French government also has the authority to use troops to perform work left undone by strikers. Military trucks, for example, have often been used in Paris for public transportation during strikes.

Emergency situations in Britain, prior to 1971, were subject to three main provisions of British law. The Emergency Power Act of 1920 allows the government special powers after a royal proclamation of an 'emergency,' defined as an actual or threatened interference with food, water, or lighting supplies or the means of locomotion, depriving 'the community or any substantial portion of the community of the essentials of life.' The special powers include the authority to make regulations necessary to avoid the threatened deprivation and for 'purposes essential to the public safety and the life of the community'; but the regulations must immediately be submitted to Parliament for approval and cannot continue for more than seven days without a concurring resolution in both houses. If so approved, the regulations can create criminal offences, but there can be no punishment without trial. In addition, no such regulation may impose any form of compulsory military service or industrial conscription, nor make it an offence to take part in a strike or peacefully to persuade others to take part in a strike.

In 1964, the Act of 1920 was amended. Among other things, the amendments made permanent the Defence (Armed Forces) Regulations, 1939, which enable the government to use the armed forces, without consulting Parliament, on any 'urgent work of national importance,' including the employment of troops to perform work left undone by strikers.

The Conspiracy and Protection of Property Act, 1875, made it a crime for a worker employed in gas or water undertakings wilfully to break his contract of service knowing or having reasonable cause to believe that the probable consequence of his so doing would deprive the inhabitants of that area wholly or to a great extent of their water or gas supply. A 1919 statute added electricity workers to the list.

Prior to 1971, the foregoing statutes were supplemented by the power of the government to use its conciliation services or to set up a Court of Inquiry, with the power to recommend. The Industrial Relations Act, 1971, since repealed, added new emergency disputes procedures modeled after those contained in the American LMRA.

How well have the foregoing policies and procedures worked? As might be expected, those countries in which the principal bargaining parties have accepted responsibility for either avoiding emergencies or ameliorating their impact have had the greatest degree of success. To the extent that governments have relied primarily on the superior power of the state, as distinguished from the willing co-operation of the parties, they have been demonstrably less successful in preventing or coping with emergencies.

Sweden and Germany seem to have the best records in handling emergencies without active intervention by the government. In France and Britain, on the other hand, the governmental authorities have on occasion found it impossible to enforce their decrees. In 1963, the French government unsuccessfully attempted to requisition thousands of coal miners, who ignored the orders and remained on strike for six weeks. In Britain, some 22 years earlier, the British government prosecuted a thousand Kent coalminers for striking illegally in time of

war. All of the defendants pleaded guilty; most were fined, and three
leaders were sentenced to brief prison terms. After only eleven days,
however, they were released, following a visit to the jail by a government minister and the union's national secretary and the settlement
of the strike on terms demanded by the strikers.

In the United States, the emergency procedures under the RLA
worked well for a number of years, but in recent times the job security issues confronting the declining railroad industry and a breakdown of effective collective bargaining led to a series of threatened
national railroad strikes and a series of *ad hoc* interventions by Congress in the form of special legislation to deal with particular disputes.
Taft-Hartley emergency procedures are generally regarded by specialists in the field as unnecessary in most disputes and ineffective in true
emergencies. Yet there is no urgent demand for reform of this legislation because it is invoked so seldom – on an average of about once a
year since 1948. In short, the vitality of private-sector collective bargaining in the United States has virtually obviated the need to resort
to the Taft-Hartley emergency-disputes procedures.

INTERESTS DISPUTES IN GOVERNMENT EMPLOYMENT

The distinction observed in the private sector between run-of-the-mill
disputes and emergency disputes is much more difficult to draw in
the case of government employment. The reason is that any interruptions of government services, regardless of their impact on the local
or national community, tend to be regarded as emergencies by large
segments of the public. In part this reaction results from the feeling
that the sovereign powers of government are being challenged, and
that the mere challenge constitutes an emergency. From this point of
view, every strike by government employees, regardless of the reason,
is a political strike. Yet in many situations the reality hardly corres-
ponds with the perception. Even assuming that any strike against the
government implicitly rejects the extreme claims of sovereignty, it
does not necessarily follow that all strikes of government employees
are challenges to the political system. In the majority of instances,
they are attempts to obtain the same kinds of improved wages, hours,
and working conditions as those for which workers strike in the private sector; and, frequently, public service strikes should logically be
a cause for much less concern than those in the private sector. In the
United States, for example, some government agencies carry out large-

ly proprietary functions, whereas many so-called public utilities are privately owned. Moreover, it cannot be denied that the general public has a greater need for uninterrupted production in a major private industry, such as coal or steel, than for continuous service in some minor government activity, such as the care of grass and shrubbery in public parks.

Nevertheless, the law in the United States, and in most other countries as well, has, until relatively recently, applied one standard to strikes by employees in private industry and another to strikes by government employees. In the United States, with few exceptions, the latter are denied the right to strike, either by statute or by judicial decisions. The basic reasons for this double standard were recently stated by a three-judge federal district court in the Postal Clerks case: 'Given the fact that there is no constitutional right to strike, it is not irrational for the Government to condition employment on a promise not to withhold labour collectively, and to prohibit strikes by those in public employment, whether because of the prerogatives of the sovereign, some sense of higher obligation associated with public service, to assure the continuing functioning of the Government without interruption, to protect public health and safety or for other reasons.'

The theory thus expressed is not peculiar to the United States. The Swedish scholar, Stig Jägerskiöld, writes: 'For many years it was said in Sweden, as well as in other northern countries, that a full labour law system could not properly be applied within the field of public administration. It was argued that the introduction of the collective agreement in public service [and, *a fortiori*, the right to strike] would be contrary to the concept of state sovereignty and would unduly restrict the power of decision which the authorities must be able to exercise. It could eventually give rise to obligations of public officials toward their associations that would bind them improperly and impair their loyalty to the state or the local government.'

Speaking of the German *Beamter* (for whom it is impossible to find a closer description than the admittedly inexact term, 'public official') Professor William H. McPherson remarks: 'Considering his relationship of service and loyalty to the state, it is quite 'inconceivable' that he might strike against the state. The incongruity of such action was felt to be so clear that it was considered unnecessary and inappropriate to spell out a strike prohibition in the public law. This is still the prevailing view although a few labour law specialists have recently challenged it ... ' *Beamte*, however, occupy a different status from public service employees, whose right to strike after reaching a deadlock in negotiations is unquestioned.

In France, prior to 1946, civil servants (*fonctionnaires*) and public service employees (*salariés des services publics*) were denied the right to organize in unions, to bargain collectively, or to strike. According to Professor Frederic Meyers, 'the Conseil d'Etat seemed to read into the right of organization the right to strike which, it held, was 'incompatible with the essential continuity of national life.' '

In most countries, however, the attitude toward strikes and other forms of industrial action by government employees had undergone considerable change in recent years. Among the group of countries discussed in this paper, the United States has been the slowest to modify the rules applicable to government employees. Federal employees are still forbidden by law to strike under any circumstances. Only seven states (Vermont, Montana, Pennsylvania, Hawaii, Alaska, Minnesota, and Oregon) grant even a limited right to strike to their employees.

In Sweden, prior to enactment of the State Officials and Municipal Officials Acts of 1965, strikes by Swedish public officials were held to be violations of the penal code and punishable by fine, dismissal, or imprisonment. But public officials found different ways to exert pressure, including resigning *en masse* and boycotting vacancies. Jägerskiöld notes that such offensive actions 'have been used to a far greater extent than would be presumed if only existing legal rules prohibiting strikes were considered.' And he adds: 'The steps taken in recent years by the Norwegian, Swedish, and Finnish governments to permit coercive measures are thus not so radical as they might at first seem. In these countries it was thought that to elaborate a legal system in which strikes and lockouts have their well-defined place may be advantageous.'

The State Officials Act was adopted on condition that the principal unions representing state officials enter into the Basic Agreement of 1966 establishing special procedures for disputes potentially dangerous to society. Collective bargaining is confined to questions of remuneration and related employment conditions; other matters, such as distribution of work, size of work force, and hours of work, are reserved to the unilateral determination by the state. Lawful industrial action (strike or lockout only) is limited to issues subject to collective bargaining, and no strike is legal unless officially declared by a trade union.

Provisions for dealing with disputes potentially dangerous to society are not established by statute, but are incorporated in collective agreements between government authorities and the unions representing state officials. Under both the State Officials and the Municipal Officials Acts, bipartite Public Service Councils were created, each side having equal representation. Only one of these parties (not another 'public authority') may raise the claim that a dispute is one 'calculated unduly to disturb important social functions.' This claim, once raised, creates an obligation to negotiate in order to 'avoid, limit, or end the dispute.' In the union's case, this may mean an agreement that a certain proportion of its members will not strike. If negotiations fail to bring agreement, the matter must be referred to the Public Service Council, and any 'offensive action' of which notice has been given must be postponed for as long as three weeks. If the Council, by majority vote, pronounces a dispute socially dangerous, the party concerned is put under strong pressure to limit or end the dispute.

However, in the widespread disputes in 1971, between the Swedish National Collective Bargaining Office and several unions representing various state and municipal employees over the government and LO policy aimed at equalizing incomes, the government was forced, for the first time, to intervene with *ad hoc* legislation extending lapsed collective agreements for a maximum of six weeks. This action was taken after certain state officials, railway personnel, marine pilots, and municipal social workers had struck, and the National Collective Bargaining Office had retaliated by locking out thousands of other non-striking union members, including school and university teachers, and by threatening to lock out even selected groups of army officers.

In West Germany the solid consensus that *Beamte* do not have the right to strike began to erode in 1970. Although a 1922 decision to that effect by the Federal Constitutional Court is still the controlling precedent, two of three legal opinions on the point commissioned by three different unions argued in favour of a limited right to strike for *Beamte*. McPherson concludes that the complete illegality of a civil servant strike in West Germany, although generally recognized, is increasingly questioned.

In Italy the law is by no means clear. Like the German *Beamte*, some categories of employees – civil servants of the state, the police, and members of the armed services – are considered not as employees but as public officials occupying a special status. Such employees have been denied the right to organize in trade unions and, of course, the right to strike. Yet a strike by municipal policemen in 1965 was excused on the ground that they were honestly mistaken about their legal rights to organize and to strike. In 1969 the Constitutional Court limited the scope of the provision in the penal code previously referred to, holding that it unconstitutionally interfered with the right of employees in the public service to strike to achieve legitimate 'socio-economic objectives.'

In France, as previously noted, the courts have accepted as valid statutory or regulatory limitations upon the right to strike of particular groups, including policemen, judges, prison wardens, and air-controllers. Each minister may by way of regulation (*arrêté* or *circulaire*) place limitations upon the right to strike in public service enterprises which come under his authority. Such limitations have been applied to the railways, public transport in Paris, and to the post office. Regulations have required notice of strike action or prohibited certain types of strike, such as *grèves tournantes* (rotating or rolling strikes).

A 1963 law placed some restrictions upon public employees working for the state or for departments or communes with more than 10,000 inhabitants, and workers in public service industries. First, strikes by their employees on less than five days' notice are now unlawful; moreover, notice may be given only by the 'most representative' of the trade unions in the affected enterprise or service. Second, all *grèves tournantes* are unlawful. Participation in such strikes by civil servants and public service employees is considered to be *faute lourde*. Those engaging in repeated short strikes of less than one day's duration may nevertheless be fined one day's pay. The law has been vigorously opposed by union leaders, and it has not been consistently enforced. Indeed, the agreements settling the 1968 strikes expressly included clauses providing that the law in this regard would not be enforced.

Only in Britain has the civil servant or public official not been singled out for special treatment in strike law. Similarly, employees of public corporations are not regarded as different from other employees. The government has encouraged membership in trade unions by its employees and has voluntarily entered into collective agreements with them. Although the government and various unions vol-

untarily agreed to submit disputes for binding determination by a tripartite Civil Service Arbitration Tribunal, strikes by government employees have become increasingly common in recent years, and have
involved teachers, ambulance personnel, hospital workers, firefighters,
naval dockyard workers, municipal dustmen and sewage workers, and
postal workers. None of these strikes gave rise to legal sanctions. Thus,
it appears that in Britain the right of virtually all government employees to strike is taken for granted. The principal exceptions appear to
be the armed forces and the police.

SUBSTITUTES FOR STRIKE AND LOCKOUT
IN INTERESTS DISPUTES

Compulsory arbitration
The most common substitute for resort to strike or lockout in interests disputes is compulsory arbitration. This procedure may take various forms: it may be automatic upon the failure of preliminary conciliation; it may be mandatory upon submission of either party,
regardless of the consent of the other party; or it may be imposed by
the government on its own motion and within its sole discretion, on
an *ad hoc* basis.

Compulsory arbitration has been an integral part of the industrial
relations systems of Australia and New Zealand for many years. It was
used in Germany after the First World War and in France for a few
years before the Second World War. It was resorted to during wartime
in both Britain and the United States, and it has been adopted by a
number of states in the United States for government employees. In
Canada it is currently one form of interests-dispute resolution available to federal employees covered by the Public Service Staff Relations Act, and it is prescribed for certain groups of provincial employees such as the Ontario municipal police force.

The Australian system is too complicated to describe in this paper,
but two observations on its operation must be made. First, in actual
practice, the process under the Conciliation and Arbitration Act involves a good deal of bargaining by employers and unions with each
other and with the Conciliation and Arbitration Commission, especially in respect of the application of the awards. Second, although
strikes are outlawed, Australia has consistently had one of the highest
strike rates in the world.

It is in the sector of government employment that we can observe the greatest tolerance by employees of compulsory arbitration as a substitute for the strike. The preference of most Canadian federal employees for compulsory arbitration, in place of the alternative of engaging in a strike after exhausting compulsory conciliation, has been widely noted. In the United States, many groups of organized employees, especially police and firefighters, have publicly favoured compulsory arbitration over the right to strike, and statutes in a number of states provide for compulsory arbitration of interests disputes involving those specific groups.

The experience in the United States at the state, county, and municipal levels of government employment has been especially interesting. The renunciation of the right to strike, at least by some affiliates of the AFL-CIO, has been relatively recent. It has been accompanied by the abandonment by many groups of local government employers – the League of California Cities, for example – of their former position of unalterable opposition to the right of any government employees to strike. Less than ten years ago, the League urged compulsory arbitration as the only acceptable method of resolving interests disputes in government employment. Today, as the issue is being debated in the California legislature, where a proposed comprehensive collective bargaining law for government employees is under discussion, the cities and counties of California are united in their opposition to compulsory arbitration, but are apparently reconciled to the inevitability of a law granting at least a limited right to strike to government employees.

The principal argument against compulsory arbitration of interests disputes has traditionally been that it undermines collective bargaining. It is alleged that in the earlier stages of negotiations the parties merely 'go through the motions' of bargaining and are less concerned about reaching agreement than about preparing their positions for compulsory arbitration. Moreover, especially in the United States, where both management and labour are strongly opposed to compulsory arbitration in the private sector, there is great fear that such a procedure would make virtually inevitable considerably greater control by government over the private economy than it presently exercises.

Undoubtedly, there is considerable justification for both those concerns. But the newly expressed opposition by government employers to compulsory arbitration reflects a different fear, based upon compulsory arbitration decisions on economic issues in some of the nation's major cities. A few of these awards have been described by the government agencies involved as ruinous, and as imposing obligations upon them far in excess of their ability to pay. The danger perceived by public management is that arbitrators lacking sufficient knowledge of the workings of municipal government will increasingly impose upon elected officials a system of priorities inconsistent with the mission of the various public agencies. Moreover, in the last five to ten years, a number of cities and counties in the United States have experienced strikes by various groups, including police and firefighters, and have discovered that, contrary to their former assumptions, the consequences were substantially less than catastrophic.

These developments also explain a diminishing interest by some groups of government employees in the right to strike. Police and firefighters have done very well so far under compulsory arbitration, although the trend toward large awards, which were largely based on the need to establish parity or some reasonable relationship with wages and fringe benefits paid to other groups, is rapidly coming to an end. In addition, the relatively few state laws permitting government employees to strike are hedged with so many preliminary procedural requirements and other limitations that many labour organizations consider them to be virtually useless. Finally, powerful unions have, so far, been able to strike illegally without incurring serious penalties, while weak unions are likely to profit little if any from a statutory right to strike.

Ironically, as government employers in the United States evidence growing disenchantment with both compulsory and voluntary arbitration of interests disputes, there is some movement in the private sector toward substituting voluntary arbitration for the strike. The most conspicuous example of this development, which is as yet no more than a straw in the wind, and certainly not a trend, is the 1974 Experimental Negotiating Agreement in the steel industry. Having concluded that the periodic strikes in the industry have cost more than they were worth, the parties agreed to begin negotiations over the terms of their 1974 contract ahead of the normal schedule, and to conclude those negotiations several months before the expiration of their previous contract. They further agreed that at the end of the negotiation period, all unresolved issues would be submitted to binding arbitration. This experiment resulted in the disposition of all issues through collective bargaining, thus obviating the need for arbitration; and the parties were so pleased with the arrangement that they agreed to adopt it the next time their contract is open for renewal.

Other options
1. Final-offer selection. The absence of a pre-emptive federal statute covering collective bargaining by government employees in the United

States has led to a rich and imaginative development of impasse-resolution procedures in interests disputes in the several States. Perhaps the most popular of these procedures is some form of final-offer selection. The theory underlying this device is based on several assumptions, including the belief that arbitrators are, by nature, compromisers who will never decide an issue on the 'merits' if they can split the difference, and the belief that whereas conventional compulsory arbitration 'chills' collective bargaining, final-offer selection forces the parties to engage in hard and realistic bargaining.

Final-offer selection compels the selectors to choose between the final offers submitted by the parties, and prohibits the selectors from modifying the offer or offers so chosen. This, presumably, acts as an effective restraint on the tendency to issue compromise awards. The risk to the losing party is considerable, hence the assumption that each side will make its final offer as reasonable as possible in the hope of forestalling its rejection in favour of the other side's final offer.

In the United States there are at present six jurisdictions that provide for final-offer selection; half of these are limited to firefighters and police. In all cases the employees covered are denied the right to strike. The best known laws are those of Wisconsin and Michigan, both of which are limited to firefighters and police.

Under the Michigan law, disputes over economic issues which are not resolved within thirty days of their submission to mediation or fact-finding (or within additional periods agreed to by the parties) may be submitted to final-offer selection by a tripartite panel at the request of either party. Economic issues in dispute are identified by the panel, and each party must, within prescribed time limits, but after the hearing before the panel, submit its last offer of settlement on each issue. Within thirty days after conclusion of the hearing, the panel must adopt the 'last offer of settlement which, in the opinion of the panel, more nearly complies with the [eight] applicable factors' prescribed in the law. The chairman of the panel, if he thinks it would be beneficial to do so, is also empowered to remand the dispute to the parties for further bargaining for a period not to exceed three weeks at any time before rendering the award.

The Wisconsin law permits the parties a choice between conventional arbitration and final-offer selection. If the latter method is selected to resolve the dispute, each party is permitted to amend its final offer at any time up to five days before the date of the hearing.

The criteria which the final-offer selector must consider are identical with those in the Michigan law. The principal difference between the two statutes is that Michigan permits final-offer selection on an issue-by-issue basis, whereas Wisconsin requires that final offers on all issues be included in a single package.

The City of Eugene, Oregon, was the first jurisdiction in the United States to try final-offer selection. Its 1971 ordinance requires both parties to file their final offers (a final offer and an alternative one) with the city recorder if agreement is not reached on the terms of a collective agreement within 25 days after the commencement of negotiations. These four offers may constitute a complete proposed agreement or may be limited to the specific items still in dispute. If agreement is not reached within the succeeding five days, the final offers are forwarded to the final selection board; if only disputed issues are submitted, all items previously agreed to must be filed with the recorder. Continuing negotiations between the parties until the final-selection board has rendered its decision are encouraged. The board members are prohibited from attempting to mediate the dispute, but the board is not precluded from 'obtaining whatever information from whatever sources it deems appropriate to assist in its selection.' The final selection must be made within ten days from submission of the final offers, and must be based on four criteria specified in the ordinance.

Experience under these various forms of final-offer selection, though still too meagre to support firm conclusions, does suggest several hypotheses. First, a tripartite panel given power to select final offers on an issue-by-issue basis is more likely to produce an acceptable settlement than a single person who must choose between two 'packages,' consisting of final offers on a number of different issues. Success will also be enhanced if the parties do not have to submit their final offers until after the hearing at which they explain their respective positions, and if they are also given the opportunity to resume bargaining for a few more days following submission of their final offers. The Michigan experience suggests that in this final period of bargaining the parties have a better than even chance of reaching an agreement. The reason for this is readily apparent. Under the Michigan procedure, the interaction among the members of the tripartite panel and between them and the parties amounts to a kind of mediation and tends to minimize the differences between the parties as their expectations become more realistic. Agreement reached in the final bargaining stages thus represents a mutual acceptance of what is likely to be the outcome of final selection.

2. 'Med-arb.' This procedure, a combination of mediation and arbitration, has aroused somewhat more interest in the United States than it perhaps deserves. The same process in Britain has been more felicitously described by Wedderburn and Davies as ' 'rolling conciliation,' with pauses for arbitral breath.' In brief, the procedure is one in which a person or panel is engaged to mediate a series of disputed issues and to arbitrate those which the parties fail to settle. It can work only if the parties are determined to reach agreement, but require third-party intervention either because they have run out of ideas or because one or both of them need to blame an inevitable result on someone else. (As Harry Shulman, the first umpire under the Ford Motor Co. – United Auto Workers agreement once observed, 'saving face' is important to the parties, and the arbitrator's face is always expendable for that purpose.) Moreover, the person or panel selected must have the complete trust of both sides – a situation that does not occur frequently.

A much more common and effective procedure might be called 'arb-med.' In those jurisdictions, such as New York, which have adopted compulsory arbitration as the means of resolving interests disputes, it appears that arbitrators do mediate, often effectively. These activities are informal and are tailored to the individual situation. They are not part of the statutory procedure and may, indeed, be contrary to its intent. Nevertheless, they often work, resulting either in a narrowing of differences or a voluntary settlement of the dispute.

3. Binding fact-finding. The State of Nevada initiated in 1971 a unique experiment for settling interests disputes between local governments and their employees. The existing law was amended to give the governor authority, at the request of either party to a dispute, and prior to the commencement of fact-finding proceedings, to order the fact-finder's award binding on any or all issues. The governor's decision must take into account 'the overall best interests of the state and all its citizens,' the 'potential fiscal impact both within and outside the political subdivision,' and 'any danger to the safety of the people of the state or a political subdivision.' In addition, the fact-finder, whether serving in an advisory or arbitral capacity, must make a preliminary determination of the local government's financial ability

to pay, based on 'all existing revenues as established by the local government employer,' and with 'due regard for the obligation of the
local government employer to provide facilities and services guarantee-
ing the health, welfare, and safety of the people residing within the
political subdivision.' Once ability to pay is found, the fact-finder is
directed to use 'normal criteria for interest disputes' in arriving at his
recommendation or decision.

The governor's decision-making process under the Nevada statute
has two principal features. The first is unpredictability; his twenty-
two decisions so far (1972-73) cannot be accounted for by application of any declared or readily observable formula. The second feature
is the element of judgment as to the reasonableness of the parties'
respective bargaining positions, taking into consideration, on economic issues, the financial position of the local government employer.
Both features are apparently well understood by the parties, and were
partly responsible for the approximately nine settlements reached before the governor had to make a decision. Moreover, even if the governor orders binding fact-finding, the costs of the fact-finder's services,
legal fees, transcripts, etc., plus the fear of an adverse decision, tend
to encourage settlement before commencement of fact-finding proceedings. In 1973, of the eight cases sent by the governor to binding
fact-finding on some or all issues, four were settled prior to commencement of the hearing.

The Nevada experiment, although of some interest, is obviously
not one that is likely to be tried in many other jurisdictions. It is cited
simply as further evidence of the wide variety of experimentation
with interests disputes settlement procedures that is being conducted
in the United States.

CONCLUSIONS

In a recent issue of the *New Yorker*, the American political and economic analyst, Richard N. Goodwin, addressed himself to the current
economic crisis in the United States and the failure of established
economic theory to deal effectively with it. He began his 'Reflections'
with a scientific analogy: 'As the earth was fixed at the centre of the
universe, the task of astronomy in the ancient world was to describe
the movement of the other planets and the stars. It would have been
more aesthetic – and in later times more helpful to theological per-
suasion – to assume a model of the universe in which the heavenly

bodies moved in perfect circular dignity about the terrestrial focus. The ancients, however, would not allow dogma or preconception to rule or distort the facts of observation; some stars, for example, seemed to change their speed, others to temporarily reverse direction and then resume a normal course. God's universe was more complex than man might wish but not, certainly, too intricate for man's understanding. Gradually, astronomers constructed a model of the universe in which stars and planets moved around each other while moving around the earth: circles within circles within circles; cycles and epicycles – all rotating in one grand design. As new irregularities were observed, the model was modified: an orbit added, relationships adjusted. This system, known as the Ptolemaic, after the greatest of its builders, lasted for fourteen centuries, until Copernicus hypothesized: What if, for the sake of argument, we assume that the earth moves around the sun? In his great work, "On the Revolutions of the Celestial Orbs," he propounded no decisive new evidence, recorded no observations that could not be explained by the Ptolemaic system. But he asked the right question.' Is it possible that there is a 'Copernican question' waiting to be formulated in respect of the settlement of interests disputes in the essential and public sectors?

It may well be that such a question has already been asked. In his book, *Droit Social*, published in 1968, Professor Gerard Lyon-Caen declared: 'The Accords de Grenelle for the first time rightly joined together in the same document relating to civil servants [*fonctionnaires*], employees in the public sector and employees in the private sector. Should we not draw from this fact certain conclusions as to the unity of Labour Law? ... Why not decide that the whole of Labour Law is applicable to the public sector?'

Yesterday, Professor Boivin seemed to be asking a similar question. Whether 'the whole of Labour Law' can ever be applied to the public sector in countries such as the United States and Canada is highly problematical. Although opinions differ widely on the extent of the differences between the private and the public sectors in these countries, the consensus is that some important differences do exist. Among those most frequently cited are the absence of a profit motive, the greater security of employment, the lower elasticity of demand for services, the relative lack of substitutes for those services, and the relatively higher degree of accountability in the public sector. To be sure, all of these alleged differences have been challenged on various grounds, but people generally, at least in the United States, are convinced that government service is substantially different from private employment.

The question raised by Lyon-Caen is more pertinent, however, in Britain, where it seems to a large extent already to have been answered in the affirmative, and in the other European democracies, where the so-called private economy has become increasingly socialized. In France, for example, nationalized enterprises or those controlled by the government are expected to set standards that will be followed by privately owned enterprises.

The question is still more pertinent and of broader application if it is limited to the settlement of interests disputes in the essential and public sectors. Here we have already seen tendencies in all of the countries mentioned for the applicable laws in the public and private sectors to become increasingly similar. In all of these countries the private sector appears to have provided the model, but in the United States we may in time see a reversal of that pattern. It is no longer true, and has not been for some time, that legislative experiments in the public sector conducted by individual states can be confined, to use Justice Holmes' phrase, to the 'insulated chambers' within their geographical boundaries. The walls of separation have become, at the very least, semipermeable membranes, and some state statutes seem to have been absorbed by the statutes of other states by what might be termed a process of legislative osmosis. And because virtually all state experimentation in the private sector has been precluded by the LMRA, new ideas for handling interests disputes have necessarily been limited to the public sector. One or more of those which prove successful may eventually be adopted for use in federal laws applicable to the private sector.

It appears, too, that traditional views that strikes in the public sector – especially strikes by public officials with a special status, such as the German *Beamte* – are not to be tolerated, are beginning to change. In the United States, for example, there is a growing awareness of what Sweden has already discovered; that providing for a limited right to strike may more effectively prevent illegal industrial action than will outright prohibition.

So much for this astigmatic glance into a cloudy future. One feels a greater confidence in reaffirming, on the basis of hard evidence, an observation made by Kahn-Freund and many others (including Professor Phillips and Mr Matkin) that law itself can play but a limited role in the settlement of interests disputes in the essential and public sectors. At best, it can provide a framework or procedure for the use of the parties; but legal sanctions against violations of law will never effectively prevent such violations if employees, whether in the private or public sectors, become convinced that they are being treated unfairly and that only a resort to self-help offers any hope of relief.

The possibility suggested yesterday by Dean Peitchinis, that perhaps the way to deal with strikes in the public sector is to explore the methods and costs of removing the causes of such strikes recalls what has always seemed to me the hopeless quest of Elton Mayo and his disciples for the golden formula that will bring about the 'spontaneous collaboration' between managers and employees. For reasons suggested at the outset of my paper, I do not think it likely that reasons for strikes, or strikes themselves, can ever be eliminated. This means that private arrangements to protect the public's interests – whether undertaken bilaterally by the bargaining parties, as in Sweden, or unilaterally by the unions, as in West Germany – are more effective than statutory procedures and sanctions. But if that is indeed the case, the outlook for the responsible resolution of interests disputes in the United States is not particularly roseate, at least in the immediate future.

The immense size of the United States, the diversity of its industry and trade, the traditions of competition and of employer hostility to unionism, and the decentralized character of collective bargaining all combine to prevent even the possibility of basic agreements on key policies of labour-management relations being reached by representatives of the two groups, as has been the case in Sweden. Indeed, there are in the United States no organizations remotely comparable to the SAF and the LO. In the public sector matters are worse. Whereas in the private sector, some forty years of collective bargaining have substantially moderated the grosser forms of industrial conflict and have prepared the way for such significant innovations as the Experimental Negotiating Agreement in the steel industry, few areas in the public sector reflect any of these evolutionary developments. With some notable exceptions, government managers in the United States, especially at county and municipal levels, remain almost totally ignorant of the theory and operation of collective bargaining systems in both the private sector and the few areas of the public sector where they have been established. By their hostility to shared decision-making, their fear of any organization calling itself a union, their unswerving allegiance to their own omniscience in interpreting and carrying out the 'missions' of their respective agencies, and their total rejection of academic research which concedes even the slightest similarity between the public and private sectors, these managers have preserved for themselves a totally unreal world, as remote from the present situation as was the world of private employers in the 1930s. Of course, having resolutely refused to learn anything from the mistakes made by private employers when collective bargaining was unceremoniously thrust upon them, these public managers are doomed to repeat them. But one way or another, either voluntarily or kicking and screaming against their will, government employers are eventually going to come to terms with collective bargaining. I agree completely with Professor Boivin that the process now taking place is irreversible.

DISCUSSION

Aaron I thought it might be worthwhile to hit quickly some of the main points I tried to make in the paper. Like Professor Phillips, and I suppose the other two speakers as well, I got my marching orders from Professor Beatty and I took my title from his letter. You'll notice it speaks of interest disputes in the essential and public services. Now to me that suggested the assumption that all public services are essential, although maybe that was not his intent. In any case, I say in my paper that I don't think all public services are essential. I might add, parenthetically, although I didn't directly address myself to this in the paper, that I'm a little weary of trying to classify services in order of essentiality or near essentiality, in the manner attempted by Professor Phillips in his paper. There always seems to be something that is forgotten. Alaska recently adopted a law in which it set up three categories: one of absolute essentiality, one of sufficient importance so that there had to be some restriction on the right to strike, and a third for all others. But I understand that one service not included in the first two classes turned out to be as important as the most essential services – one that we would have known all about in a city such as Los Angeles: that is, the social workers who fill out and mail the welfare cheques. Now I cite that merely as an example of the kind of thing that can happen if you try to set out in a statute certain categories in some order of importance. It's like a criminal statute; you're always forgetting some thing; there has to be a loop-hole that needs to be plugged up.

Well, anyway, I began with a brief introductory discussion of the distinction between disputes over rights and disputes over interests, which I introduced solely to point out that observance or non-observance of that distinction is reflected in the incidence of strikes and in the procedures for settling them. I then turned to questions of essentiality and emergency. I define an emergency dispute as one in which the disputants can hold out longer than the public is either able or willing to do. And using the emergency disputes procedures under the Taft-Hartley and Railway Labor Acts in the United States as examples, I attempt to show, as Harry Arthurs observed yesterday and as others have also pointed out, that questions of essentiality and emergency, although theoretically subject to objective determination, are in fact always controlled by political considerations. In the United States we say that despite the definition in the Taft-Hartley Act of an emergency – a threatened or actual strike or lockout imperilling the national health or safety – it is whatever the President of the United States says it is. And in that connection, I tried to show that the procedures in the Taft-Hartley Act are totally silly and unavailing, but that it makes no difference because the state of collective bargaining in that sector of the economy which is covered by that statute is sufficiently healthy so that the existence or non-existence of the Taft-Hartley Act makes no difference. In contrast, the procedures under the Railway Labor Act make a great deal of sense but appear to be working very poorly because of the intractability of the kinds of problems now confronting the railroad industry and the resultant breakdown in collective bargaining procedures in that industry. I also offered the suggestion in the paper that for somewhat unconvincing reasons there has been in a number of countries, at least initially, a greater willingness to tolerate incipient emergencies in the private sector than in the public sector. I next reviewed the experience of several European countries in dealing with emergency disputes in the private sector. I noted the policy of voluntarism pursued bilaterally in Sweden by agreement between the Swedish Employers Federation and the Labour Federation, and unilaterally by the unions in Germany, and the policy of government intervention adopted in Italy and France, and more conservatively in Britain. I concluded that voluntarism, if achievable, will work better than interventionism, which is not exactly a revolutionary observation.

Turning then to interest disputes in government employment, I summarized the approaches taken in the United States and in the five European countries previously mentioned; on the basis of this evidence, I draw three principal conclusions, none of which, again, is very surprising. First, there seems to be a trend toward greater toleration of strikes and related industrial action in the public sectors, except that in the United States this trend is barely perceptible and is proceeding much more slowly than in the European countries. Second, there is some reason to believe that a law permitting some sorts of strikes by government employees is likely to result in fewer illegal strikes or other forms of industrial action, such as mass resignations, boycotting, picketing, working to rule, and so forth, than there would be if all strikes were outlawed: in other words, the safety valve may work better than an outright prohibition. Third, I concluded that punitive sanctions against illegal strikes don't work anyway. Finally, I considered various substitutes for the strike and the lockout, in interests disputes, including compulsory arbitration, involuntary arbitration, final offer selection, fact-finding, with or without recommendations, and so forth. My discussion of this topic is obviously very superficial; it doesn't purport to be anything but that. My purpose was simply to show the rich variety of experimentation now going on in the United States. That is a very rough summary of what I said in the paper.

I have no solutions to offer. I didn't come here expecting to solve your problems, any more than I expected to hear answers that could solve our problems in the United States. I shall just mention, because we haven't talked about it, what we have proposed for the settlement of interest disputes in the State of California in the bill now pending. We have proposed that when a bargaining impasse is reached between a public employer and an employee organization representing its employees, that the parties be compelled (but only if they refuse to do so themselves) to enter into mediation. If mediation, after a fixed period of time, proves unavailing, the parties then move to the next stage, which is fact-finding by a tripartite panel. The fact-finding panel is expressly given the authority and the duty to continue the mediation while it is also learning the positions of the parties in respect of the issues in dispute. And plenty of opportunity is given to the parties to continue their own bargaining while this process is going on, the idea being that there will be a continual interchange of information and communication about how the panel is leaning on the issues in dispute. Indeed, it is expected that, as in most tripartite situations, the chairman of the panel will be mediating between the partisan members, who in turn will be in touch with their principals; so by the time the proceeding is over, both sides should have a pretty good idea of what the panel is going to recommend. The panel then issues its recommendations to the parties, who are given further time, before the recommendations are made public, to try to bargain out a settlement based on the recommendations of the panel. If that fails, the parties must then decide whether they will accept the recommendations of the panel. The government employer must do so at a public hearing. It must first allow the members of the public to express their own views on what the employer should do; then it must take a roll call vote on whether to accept or reject. The employee organization, on the other hand, must conduct its vote by secret ballot. If both parties accept the fact-finding recommendations, then of course that ends the matter. If either side rejects, the other may serve notice of intent to impose a lockout. Following a minimum period of notice, the strike or walkout may take place. Thereafter, if the public employment relations board concludes that the strike or lockout imminently threatens the public health or safety, it can go into court and seek an injunction against the strike or lockout. And any interested party may appear before the court (no *ex parte* proceedings are allowed) and argue for or against the granting of the injunction. If the court decides that the injunction must issue, it must at the same time order into effect the recommendations of the fact-finding panel; so that one way or another the dispute is brought to a conclusion.

Now, that's the proposal. I don't think it has one chance in a hundred of being adopted, and it may help to show the difficulty of the problem, at least as it exists in a not unrepresentative state of the United States, to explain what the various positions are on this. The public employers do not want any aspect of compulsion in the process. What they object to is not the right to strike, but the provision that the court, if it enjoins the strike, must impose the terms of the fact-finding panel's recommendations. The legislators, on the other hand, are all for the compulsion part of it, but cannot bring themselves to vote in favour of even a very limited right to strike. And by the way, this right to strike is accompanied by, in addition to all the other restrictions that I've mentioned, other language saying that all secondary strikes are illegal. The unions are divided. Some don't want the right to strike at all, want it out of the bill, and want compulsory arbitration; others would like to have the unlimited right to strike but can't accept the idea of an injunction; and others would take the right to strike provided that there is compulsion somewhere down the line, in the manner I have indicated.

I don't think there's any particular virtue in this proposal of ours, except that it hasn't been tried anywhere else. It is merely another example of some of the experimentation that's going on. I would support it on the ground that, properly used, the fact-finding process can produce a high level of settlements without the need of any fact-finding recommendations being made at all. That is the conclusion I draw from the Michigan experience with final-offer selection on somewhat the same basis. Chuck Rhemus reports that something better than 30 per cent of the cases end in a settlement, without the need of the panel to make any final-offer selections at all.

I want to make one other comment which is admittedly somewhat irrelevant to this discourse. There have been a number of suggestions made to the effect that all the militancy has gone out of the American labour movement, that it has rolled over and played dead, and that the absence of a high level of strikes suggests that collective bargaining is dead at 28. That was Paul Jacobs' remark. When George Meany heard it, he said, 'Well, Jacobs is connected with the University of California where they have a doctrine of "publish or perish." From my point of view, there's been entirely too much publishing and not enough perishing.'

Paul has been both right and wrong on a lot of matters. I think he was absolutely wrong about this. Collective bargaining is flourishing and the labour movement in the United States is still militant; but in my judgment the emphasis has shifted. The United States is becoming less and less the archetypical free enterprise economy and is edging toward a more socialized, welfare-oriented economy; as that happens, our unions, which are very sophisticated, have begun to realize that many of the goals they seek to achieve can no longer be accomplished through collective bargaining, but must be accomplished through political action, and their emphasis is shifting accordingly. A good deal of the drive that used to go into organizing strikes is going into organizing political campaigns and political pressure for enactment of laws such as occupational safety and health, pension reform, extension of unemployment benefits, and the like. Also, American unions, as they have always been, are part of the system; they accept the economic and social framework; they are not trying to destroy anything; and, right now, they are aware that too great a pressure for wage increases, given the state of the economy, is apt to lose jobs for their members. And that is why you see Leonard Woodcock, of all people, coming from a militant, democratic organization such as the UAW, marching to the White House, hand in hand with Henry Ford, and urging a moratorium on the use of expensive devices on automobiles designed to cut down on the amount of pollution, and tax breaks to the automobile manufacturers, the imposition of higher import duties on foreign cars, and so on. On these matters, he and Ford are hand in glove, and the reason is that they're both equally worried about jobs, about sales, and about the connection between the two. To say that this means that the American labour movement has lost its militancy is to misunderstand what is going on; because when you look at the public sector, you see so much militancy, militancy that sometimes verges on the irresponsible. In the State of Pennsylvania alone, in one year, we had 66 teacher strikes. The American Federation of State, County, and Municipal Employees, AFSCME, is the fastest growing union in the United States. It has a policy of great militancy. The number of strikes, most of which are illegal, taking place in the United States increases geometrically every year, and one certainly needn't search for militancy in that sector of the economy; it's all there. I think it's just a question of different stages of development, and the militancy that was required in the private sector in the 30s is the kind of militancy that is required in the public sector in the 70s.

Stanley When we look at alternate procedures we aren't really focusing on the question of whether or not we are looking for institutions or procedures that are uniquely suited or capable of defining or determining the public interest. Are these procedures and institutions uniquely suited to determine what is necessary for the health, safety, and security of the public? Presumably that is our objective. Furthermore, what do things like health, safety and security in the public mean? We're not really focusing on the question of whether or not we have institutions that are capable of defining the public interest or whether or not they are the proper institutions to bring those public interest considerations to bear on the settling of the disputes or the issues between labour and management in the public service sector.

Previously we discussed two procedures for handling dispute resolution in essential services. They were *ad hoc* intervention by the legislatures, and having the parties themselves bargain over how the public interest might be served or how the disputes ought to be settled. I don't know whether the legislature is uniquely suited or capable of defining the public interest in each particular dispute and bringing to bear those public interest considerations on the settlement of that particular dispute, nor whether the parties themselves are capable of adequately defining the public interest. I don't think that bargaining agents and administrators acting together are necessarily the body that is most competent to bring public interest considerations to bear on the settling of their own dispute.

Woods Could legislators define the public interest? Since it is a political question, I don't know who else can.

In my own earlier suggestion, I proposed that the parties involved, knowing their role in the public sector and the type of public service they are supplying, might conceivably be able to design in their own minds an idea of the public interest. They may then reach an agreement on the steps that are necessary to minimize the possibility of serious public suffering that could result from a breakdown in their actual negotiations in collective bargaining. My proposal was to try to depoliticize the situation as much as possible and therefore to reduce the need for government intervention. If it doesn't work then there is still a role for the legislature.

Crispo There are really three stages and I don't know how one separates them. There is the first stage of defining an essential service, whether it's privately or publicly provided, and I suspect all of us would agree that this is ultimately a political decision. The second stage involves deciding the appropriate procedures, be they solution by tribunal, by *ad hoc* legislation, or by the private parties themselves. Finally there is the question of the terms of the settlement in instances where the bargaining process breaks down. There is a difficulty in putting all three of these stages, or even two of them, into the hands of one body. I don't know how, or if, this should be done, because there are really three distinct stages.

Waisglass I would like to comment on the question of the political aspects of public interest disputes. There is a fairly important distinction to be made between two different types of public interest questions. To a large extent we have been discussing public interest aspects of procedural questions, revolving largely around the protection of third party interests against being unduly or irreparably injured from what is essentially a private fight between an employer and a union. There is a different type (and both types may be present in any single case) which does not involve procedural questions, but rather basic economic or financial issues. It is this type I find particularly troublesome. It arises where the public interest gets involved as the third party to a dispute in the form of the interests of the public treasury. Thus, what emerges is a tripartite rather than a bilateral dispute.

This is troublesome because we have designed bilateral decision-making procedures that are appropriate to the functions of collective bargaining, perceived to serve well the needs of resolving differences between two parties of interest; and we are trying to apply these procedures to situations where there are three parties of conflicting interests. I do not think the bilateral system works efficiently in those cases where the government has a direct financial interest in the outcome. For example, the public is involved in almost every railway dispute, because whatever the outcome there is always the question of cost to the public treasury. The government then is involved as a third party to the dispute, but it is represented only in its peace-making, law-making, or law-enforcing roles. Other examples are the Ontario hospitals and high schools where the public treasury was an unrepresented third-party interest in labour disputes. I draw attention to these situations to raise the question of whether or not the public treasury should be at the bargaining table as the third party of interest. The government might also be there in its other roles, as mediator or umpire. I suspect that we might reduce some tensions and confusions if we could change the system to conform to the realities that call for tripartite negotiations, where a government has a direct financial interest in a dispute between a union and an employer.

LeBel I would like to express some doubt as to the desirability of relying on political intervention. Of course, some situations have important political connotations or repercussions. Further, whenever provisions are made in legislation, there is no doubt that, under our constitutional system, the legislature always retains the power and the right to intervene at some stage. This is so, whether the procedure exists or not and whether a service is essential or not. In any political system, the power to intervene must rest somewhere; in our constitutional system, this power is vested in Parliament or in the Legislature. Thus, political interventions cannot be avoided and it is not desirable that they be avoided.

Nevertheless, I am concerned by a wholehearted reliance on the *ad hoc* approach because such an approach multiplies the number of political decisions that have to be made. It places all decisions at the political level and it may be that this entails too much reliance on the Legislature. Even if it is never possible to remove all need for *ad hoc* political intervention, it is still necessary to try and devise a collective bargaining system that will be as workable as possible and that will minimize the necessity of resorting to the ultimate political intervention.

There are other problems with the *ad hoc* approach, particularly if you look outside British Columbia, because its experience may not be typical, at least not as typical as Quebec experiences. *Ad hoc* intervention has the potential for being highly innovative and for making it possible to devise solutions that are peculiarly well adapted to the problem at hand. In practice, however, what happens may be totally different. Once political intervention occurs there are tremendous pressures for using that solution more frequently; governments become intervention-prone. Furthermore, instead of being innovative, the solutions which are legislated have a way of becoming totally stereotyped. The federal solution appears to be to legislate the return to work and to provide for some sort of mediation backed up by compulsory arbitration for the remaining issues in dispute. In Quebec, legislative intervention has also been highly stereotyped. It has provided substantial penalties directed against unions, union officers, or workers who continue to engage in illegal strikes.

I would suggest that it is entirely possible to retain the advantages of an extremely flexible approach to emergency disputes, which we all agree is desirable, while still avoiding to a large extent the problems that are generated by wholesale reliance on *ad hoc* intervention. There is a solution which has not yet been discussed. Although I have never really been a great fan of the 'arsenal of weapons' approach, it appears to be the only solution to these problems. In such a situation, power is given to some authority to choose between the various types of interventions that are described in the legislation: return to work, compulsory arbitration, cooling-off period, etc. Resorting to any one solution does not prevent legislative intervention. Hopefully, however, in many situations legislative intervention would be unnecessary.

I would also like to point out that I do share the concern over repeated ministerial intervention. The Quebec Minister of Labour, Mr Jean Cournoyer, has been inclined to intervene in labour disputes. In practice, this tends to generate the need for more frequent intervention on the part of the Minister because the public and the parties start looking to him as a 'chief fireman.' On the other hand, once the Minister has intervened, both the reputation of the government and that of the Minister are at stake. This may create quite a pressure for inflated settlements.

Fleck Based on Professor Aaron's paper, I have a great deal of difficulty in perceiving the forces that will bring the parties together in the public sector. Comparisons were made between the present militancy in the public sector and that which existed in the private sector ten to twenty years ago. It was suggested that we'll pass through the militancy stage and have something in the public sector similar to what now exists in the private sector. I don't share this view because I don't see the similarities.

Another comment I'd like to make relates to the determination of essential services. In my mind I would relate it more to the notion of public service versus non-public service. I would even relate it to the notion of obligation, a two-way obligation involving both sides. The state has an obligation to provide employment and the employee has an obligation to provide services. More and more, in fact if not in law, governments do not lay off their employees and so provide virtually assured employment. Perhaps the employees should have an obligation to ensure their services.

Aaron I'd like to give an example of forces that can bring public managers and public employees together. When we had our first major school teachers strike in Los Angeles in 1970, I had to mediate the strike, and there wasn't any money at all to play with. There was a 46 million dollar deficit, and we were trying to figure out, among other things, a set of priorities as to how money would be spent, if and when it was obtained. Using that as an opening wedge, it was possible to get the parties at least to agree that they would jointly approach the state legislature. The school board was concerned about its inability to put into effect programs it thought necessary, which were, of course, different from those which the teachers thought were necessary; but they both agreed that they needed more money, and that was one common bond. On that basis, we were able to get a first agreement that had no salary or fringe adjustments of any kind, but which did provide a few other things such as a grievance procedure and final and binding arbitration. Many issues were referred to study committees consisting of equal numbers of school board and teacher representatives, with the full understanding by the teachers that if the parties couldn't agree, the management view would prevail. Unfortunately, a court subsequently threw out the whole thing, on the ground that the school board didn't have the power to delegate any of its decision-making authority; but that is one way to put it together.

There is also the question of the dynamics that will bring about accommodation in the public sector similar to what we've had in the private sector in the last forty years. One such force is the accountability of the public agency. In time it will be more readily perceived, as comparisons are made between public jurisdictions in which collective bargaining has been established and is working reasonably well and those in which collective bargaining has not been established or is not working well, that public service in the former is more efficient and reliable than in the latter. I also think it likely that we shall have more illegal strikes in the latter group and that the public will then perceive that something is wrong. Even if it isn't completely sold on collective bargaining, it will be very apt to vote out of office the elected representatives who are responsible for that particular situation. It's a case of mutual survival, to use Wight Bakke's phrase. The need to keep the enterprise going exists, whether it is a private or a public enterprise.

One question was raised about who are the managers, and what incentives there are for management to assume a role similar to that in the private sector. Determining who is management is one of the most frustrating tasks for a newly organized group of public employees. A business agent of the Service Employees International Union once told me that the only way to uncover management was to strike and see who responded. And I think that's a very good rule of thumb. The need to develop management is in direct proportion to the extent to which public agencies are held accountable for their performance. In the United States, we have a growing awareness on the part of public management that they are being judged by the performance of their agencies, and that's our greatest hope. They are also beginning to recognize that maybe they do need a little education, and are beginning to get it in the traditional ways. They are taking courses, and learning how to form management teams and how to develop a coherent bargaining policy. As you might expect, much of this comes from people in the lower echelons; often the people at the top are still neanderthals. Those who are on the business end of things, dealing directly with employees, know that they have to do something and that some changes must be made.

A question was raised as to whether the public agency can set a different standard, based on equity rather than on pattern setting. Of course, the managers of many public agencies today apparently are harbouring the fond illusion that their system is indeed equitable because it embodies a civil service system and the merit principle, and because of constitutional or statutory obligations to follow at least the prevailing wage in the private sector. When collective bargaining comes, however, they will say: we want to bargain ourselves out from under these obligations if we can make the best deal possible. I think that the tendency may well be in exactly the opposite direction from what some suggest would be desirable. As collective bargaining takes hold, public management will think more in terms of their private-sector counterparts and try to get the best deal possible, based upon the power situation, without regard to equity.

The only concluding remark I would make is that, not surprisingly, I come away from this conference realizing, once again, that there aren't any panaceas, but more or less reassured in my belief that collective bargaining, however inadequate, is probably the instrument we're going to have to use to deal with the substantive problems we have been discussing. It's only through this continual kind of re-examination and exploration – even though it may not seem productive at the time – that we are going to be able to make the gradual and, usually, minor adjustments in the system that are necessary to keep it going.

JOHN CRISPO

Concluding remarks

Ben Aaron just said what I spend my life saying: there are no easy or quick solutions to the kinds of problems we've been discussing. Certainly no hard conclusions have emerged from this gathering. There may be some measure of agreement or consensus on some issues, but certainly not on all. In any event let me try to capture what I think may come close to some of the thinking at this seminar, putting it all as cautiously as I can.

We all seem to agree that in our present system, collective bargaining, in one form or another, is probably desirable and almost certainly inevitable in the public service as well as essential private sectors of our economy. One critical question that arises from such an assertion is how close the public service collective bargaining model should parallel the private sector model, both procedurally and in terms of substantive results. Here's where I think any agreement begins to fade.

Procedurally there was some division as to the appropriateness of the private sector model in the public sector not only because some were dubious about its present state but also because of differences in the two sectors of the economy. As you realize, I'm closer to the notion that there is nothing wrong with a parallel model. I think most of us seemed to favour this view that a somewhat similar negotiating framework is still appropriate, albeit with some differentiation to allow for the varying characteristics in the two sectors of the economy. I would argue that before we dismiss the applicability of the private model to the public sector we should at least give it a chance. For example, in the federal jurisdiction we have that confounded Public Service Staff Relations Act, which does anything but duplicate the private sector model. Indeed, if there's any double standard in this particular case, it is one that's loaded against the government, because the employees are the only ones that have a choice. As a result the weak ones go to arbitration while the others can strike with the government having no choice in the matter and in a sense being whip-sawed by the process. Furthermore, if the unions choose to strike, the government can't lock out in retaliation, if it's a partial strike or rotating strike or just plain ordinary harrassment. Worse still, it's not even clear they can lay off other workers when there is nothing for them to do because of the strike. It seems that the government doesn't have anything like the countervailing power of an employer in the private model. This being the case, I won't dismiss the private sector model, at least in the federal public service,,until it is given a better chance.

On the substantive side, there was disagreement, both in principle and in practice concerning the propriety of using private sector comparability as a major criterion in the determination of the terms and conditions of employment of public service workers. A few participants appear to favour the government as employer becoming a pattern setter, rather than a pattern follower. This notion was resisted, I believe, by a majority of those present, although some felt that this was in fact already the situation on a total net advantage or total package basis. In other words, the 'catch-up' argument may no longer be valid in some occupations and jurisdictions.

Regardless of the legislation adopted or the model chosen, the prevailing view appears to be that some work stoppages are bound to take place in public and essential services especially when inflation is rife and there is more open juggling for income shares by all organized groups in society. Some of these stoppages will invariably give rise to some public inconvenience and a certain degree of this has to be tolerated in a free society. In some instances, there will be serious harm to the public health, safety, and welfare. In these cases, we've heard over and over again that it would be preferable to have the parties themselves agree voluntarily on new procedures, or at least on measures such as partial operation to keep truly vital services operating. Government intervention in such situations should not be fixed or known in advance, otherwise the parties may allow for them in their strategies and tactics, thereby tending to undermine government intervention even before it comes into effect. Consequently, government tactical manoeuvring in these areas should feature doubt, flexibility, and uncertainty.

In this same context some mention was made of an arsenal of weapons or choice of procedures. It could be everything from fact-finding, to mediation, mediation/arbitration, mediation/final-offer selection, partial operation, to some form of voluntary or compulsory arbitration. For the most part – and here I may not be speaking for all – the right to strike or lock out should only be rescinded by special *ad hoc* legislation aimed at the restoration of absolutely critical services. Personally I think the right to strike is so basic to our collective bargaining system and to the maintenance of our free society, that it should not be abrogated except by legislation when extreme difficulties arise. Even then, we must recognize that legal sanctions have severe limitations in coping with industrial conflict where there are strong feelings about inequities, unfairness, and injustices. In the final analysis, and this came through repeatedly, politics is bound to dominate the problem of determining essential industry disputes and how they are to be handled. This is an inevitable fact of life.

In the long run, the biggest problem will be public consternation, disquiet, and intolerance of public or essential service interruptions. Indeed, there is a continuing and perhaps mounting credibility gap in our dispute resolution technique, if not in our whole collective bargaining process. A great deal of effort will be required if public opinion and pressure is not to lead our politicians to take hasty and ill-conceived action which may do more harm than good in the long run.

List of participants

GEORGE ADAMS, Vice-Chairman, Ontario Labour Relations Board,
Toronto, Ontario
TIM ARMSTRONG, Chairman, Ontario Labour Relations Board,
Toronto, Ontario
HARRY ARTHURS, Dean, Osgoode Hall Law School, York University,
Toronto, Ontario
FRANCES BAIRSTOW, Director, Industrial Relations Centre,
McGill University, Montreal, Quebec
DAVID BEATTY, Professor, Faculty of Law, and Acting Director,
Centre for Industrial Relations, University of Toronto,
Toronto, Ontario
L.W. BRAMMER, Chief Executive Officer, Labour Relations Board,
Charlottetown, P.E.I.
DON BROWN, Barrister & Solicitor, Blake, Cassels & Graydon,
Toronto, Ontario
D.D. CARTER, Professor, Faculty of Law, Queen's University,
Kingston, Ontario
A.W.R. CARROTHERS, President, Institute for Research on Public
Policy, Montreal, Quebec
INNIS CHRISTIE, Chairman, Nova Scotia Labour Relations Board,
Halifax, Nova Scotia
JOHN CRISPO, Dean, Faculty of Management Studies, University of
Toronto, Toronto, Ontario
T.M. EBERLEE, Deputy Minister of Labour, Labour Canada,
Ottawa, Ontario

J. FINKELMAN, Chairman, Public Service Staff Relations Board, Ottawa, Ontario

JAMES D. FLECK, Secretary of the Cabinet, Legislative Buildings, Queen's Park, Toronto, Ontario

PETER FREEMAN, Professor, Faculty of Law, University of Alberta, Edmonton, Alberta

D.I. GARDNER, Deputy Minister, Department of Manpower & Labour, Edmonton, Alberta

SHIRLEY GOLDENBERG, Professor, Faculty of Management, McGill University, Montreal, Quebec

MORLEY GUNDERSON, Professor, Centre for Industrial Relations, University of Toronto, Toronto, Ontario

NOEL HALL, Dean, Faculty of Commerce and Business Administration, University of British Columbia, Vancouver, B.C.

HARISH C. JAIN, Professor, Faculty of Business, McMaster University, Hamilton, Ontario

R.D. JOHNSTON, Deputy Minister, Ministry of Labour, Toronto, Ontario

ARTHUR M. KRUGER, Principal, Woodsworth College, University of Toronto, Toronto, Ontario

MARC LAPOINTE, Chairman, Canada Labour Relations Board, Ottawa, Ontario

HELENE LEBEL, Vice-Chairman, Canada Labour Relations Board, Ottawa, Ontario

NOAH M. MELTZ, Associate Chairman, Department of Political Economy, University of Toronto, Toronto, Ontario

REAL MIREAULT, Deputy Minister, Ministry of Labour and Manpower, Government of Quebec

ROBERT W. MITCHELL, Deputy Minister, Department of Labour, Regina, Saskatchewan

J. DOUGLAS MUIR, Professor, Faculty of Business Administration and Commerce, University of Alberta, Edmonton, Alberta

STEPHEN G. PEITCHINIS, Dean, Faculty of Business, University of Calgary, Calgary, Alberta

LOU PLANTJE, Director of Industrial Relations, Ministry of Labour, Winnipeg, Manitoba

J.J. REVELL, Chairman, Labour Relations Board, Charlottetown, P.E.I.

DOUGLAS C. STANLEY, Professor, Faculty of Law, University of New Brunswick, Fredericton, N.B.

CHARLES STEINBERG, Professor, Department of Economics,
Dalhousie University, Halifax, Nova Scotia

MARK THOMPSON, Acting Director, Centre for Industrial Relations,
University of British Columbia, Vancouver, B.C.

HARRY WAISGLASS,Professor, Faculty of Business, McMaster
University, Hamilton, Ontario

JAFFRAY WILKINS, Director, Pay Research Bureau, Public Service
Staff Relations Board, Ottawa, Ontario

H.D. WOODS, Professor, Faculty of Management, McGill University,
Montreal, Quebec

Lightning Source UK Ltd.
Milton Keynes UK
UKHW010000210722
406167UK00001B/255